WITHIN MY GLASS DOORS

Being a Translation of
Soseki Natsume's Garasudo-no-naka

By

Iwao Matsuhara A. B.
E. T. Iglehart, S. T. D.

With Notes

TOKYO
Shin-Sei Do
[1928]

Lincoln, Nebraska
Zea Books
2025

ISBN 978-1-60962-352-4 paperback
ISBN 978-1-60962-353-1 ebook

This English translation was originally published by
Shin-Sei Do in Tokyo in 1928.

Garasudo-no-naka 硝子戸の中 was published in 1915.

WITHIN MY GLASS DOORS

I

Looking out from within my glass doors my eye catches the banana trees covered against the frost, the holly branches laden with red berries, and a telegraph pole proudly soaring skyward. Besides these, however, there is little to be seen, and my field of vision, as I sit in my study, is most monotonous and narrowly limited. Moreover, since catching cold at the end of last year, I have hardly stepped outside, day after day sitting within my glass doors, so that I know nothing of what is going on without. I have not felt well enough to do much reading; but, now sitting, now lying, I simply note the passing of the days.

My mind has, however, sometimes been stirred, and my mood has undergone a change. Though my world be small, events sometimes occur. And within these glass doors which separate my small self from the great world, people sometimes come. These visitors have come most unexpectedly, and have done and said most unexpected things. And at times it is even with a glow of interest that I have welcomed or parted with these visitors.

I shall endeavor to commit some of this to writing. I feel that this kind of writing may seem useless in the eyes of busy men, and deem it a shame to devote much space in a precious newspaper to such impractical writings as my own, to set before readers who are too busy to do more than pull the paper from their pocket while in the tram car, and scan its headlines. These people have so little spare time that they see no necessity for newspapers, except to read of fires, robberies, murders, or such events as they regard important in the daily happenings, or such sensational news as will properly stimulate their strained nerves. They are so busy that they merely buy a paper while waiting at the tram stop, learn the world events of the previous day while taking their tram journey, and then, as soon as they reach the office the newspaper goes into their pocket, to be totally forgotten.

But still I shall write, braving the contempt of these people who have so little time at their disposal.

A great war has been going on in Europe since last year. And it seems that no one can tell when the war will come to an end. Even Japan has determined to assume a small share in it. This step now having been taken, Parliament is dissolved. The coming general election is a matter of vital importance to men in the political world. As the result of an unusual decline in the price of rice the farmers are in financial straits. Everywhere the complaint is heard, "Hard Times, Hard Times." To refer to annual events, the spring wrestling tournament is about to begin. In a word, life today is most eventful. I feel as if such a one as I, seated quietly within my glass doors, should not project himself into the newspapers. If I write, it must be to crowd out the statesmen, the military men, the business men, the wrestling fans. Naturally enough, I have not of myself the heart to undertake such a thing. But I was asked to write something this spring and will set down some unimportant items which have no connection with any but myself. How long it will continue, it is impossible now clearly to judge, for that will depend upon the facility of my pen and the editorial scissors.

II

Called to the telephone, I held the receiver to my ear and asked what was wanted. A representative of a certain magazine wanted my photograph, and asked when it would be convenient for me to have him come and take it. I replied, "I don't much like to have my photo taken."

I have never had any connection at all with this magazine. But yet I remembered having seen one or two copies of it during the past few years. Nothing remained in my mind regarding it except the many smiling faces, which I presumed might be its special feature. But I still retain the disagreeable impression caused me by these forced smiles on so many faces. And this led me to decline the request.

The magazine man said that he wished to display, in the number for January of the Year of the Rabbit, photos of those who were born in that year. There was no doubt, as he said, that I was born in the Year of the Rabbit. So I answered him, "Everyone has to pose with a smile for your magazine, doesn't he?" "No, not necessarily," he immediately replied, as though I had hitherto misunderstood the character of his magazine. "Well, if you don't mind my ordinary looks, I will accept the honor of having my photograph published." "That will be alright. Please!"

Having arranged a date with him, I hung up the receiver. The second day after, at the appointed time, the man who had called me up entered my study, dressed in fine foreign clothes, and carrying a camera. For a time we spoke about the magazine he was representing. He then took two pictures of me, one seated before my desk in my usual style, and the other standing, as I always do, in the cold frost of my garden.

The study had too poor light for pictures, so after focusing his camera he set off the magnesia flash. Just before the flash went off he turned his face partly toward me and said, "We had an agreement, but won't you smile just a bit for me?" I suddenly had a slight feeling of amusement, but at the same time I thought, What a man to say such a foolish thing! "This will do," I said, ignoring his request. When he had stood me before the tree in the garden, and directed his lens at me, again he, in the same polite style as before, repeated the words, "We had an agreement, but won't you ...?" I felt even less like laughing than before.

About four days later he sent me my photograph by mail. But the photograph had a smile on it, just as he had requested. I gazed on my own face for a while, feeling as if I had been tricked. I could not see at all how it could have been made except by some artificial means. I showed the photograph to several of my callers for their opinion. They all agreed with me in the conclusion that it was an artificial smile.

In past years it has often happened that I have forced a smile in public against my will. Perhaps these pretences took revenge through this photographer. He sent me this picture with its pained, uncanny smile, but he never sent me a copy of the magazine in which the photograph was to appear.

III

Looking back to the time when I received Hector from Mr. H., I realize that three or four years have already slipped by. It all seems to me like a dream.

At that time he was but a puppy, just weaned from his mother. A pupil of Mr. H. wrapped him in a *furoshiki* and brought him to our home in the tram car. That night I put him to sleep in a corner of the barn in the rear. To protect him from the cold I spread straw and made a bed for him, as comfortable as possible, and then closed the barn door. As soon as it grew dark he began to whine. At midnight he tried to get out by scratching down the door with his claws. Perhaps he was lonely at having to sleep by himself in the dark. He seemed not to have gotten a wink of sleep all night long.

This uneasiness continued the next night, and the night following, too. For above a week, until he at length came to sleep quietly upon the straw which I had given him, I could not get him out of my mind.

My children were much interested in him, and made a play thing of him most of their spare time. But as he had no name yet, they did not know what to call him. They felt the necessity of having a name for one with whom they had to play; so came to me with the request that I give the dog a name. At last I applied the name of Hector to this friend of my children.

This was the name of the hero of Troy, as told in the Iliad. When Troy and Greece were at war, Hector was finally overcome by Achilles, who then avenged the killing of his friend by Hector. When Achilles in rage sprang from the Grecian camp, Hector alone refused to flee into the castle. Three times Hector ran around the walls of Troy, fleeing the spear of Achilles. Three times Achilles pursued him around the walls, and finally killed him with his spear thrust. Then fastening his body to his own chariot wheels, three times again he dragged him around the walls of Troy.

I gave this mighty name to the little dog that had been brought to my home wrapped in piece of cloth. Our children, who naturally knew nothing about Hector, at first thought it a strange name. But they soon became used to it, and the dog, too, whenever the name Hector was called, responded by happily wagging his tail. By and by even this name ceased to me to have a classical sound, and became no more than such a common-place Christian name as John or George. And at the same time he gradually came to be less petted than formerly by the household.

Hector was once taken to a dog hospital because of a case of distemper, a common ailment among dogs. The children often called on him there. I too visited him. When I saw him there, he wagged his tail delightedly and turned a loving eye upon me. I crouched down and put my face close to his, and patted his head with my right hand. In gratitude he ceaselessly tried to lick my face. Then, in my presence, for the first time he drank a little milk prescribed by the physician. The physician, who hitherto had been skeptical, said that now, at this rate, he might recover. And Hector did recover. Returning home he frisked about, as lively as ever.

IV

Before long he made several friends. Among these the most intimate was a dog of about his own age, and equally mischievous, belonging to a physician just across the way. He was called John, an appropriate name for a Christian, but his character seemed far inferior to that of the heathen Hector. He had the propensity for biting everyone recklessly, and so finally ended his career by being beaten to death.

Hector often brought this evil companion into our garden, where they distracted me with their wanton destruction. They delighted in continually digging at the roots of the trees, and needlessly making great holes. They purposely rolled about upon the beautiful flower beds, scattering and destroying the precious flowers and tender plants with no compunction at all.

After John was killed, the lonely Hector learned to prowl about by day and by night. Often when I went out for a walk, I saw him basking in the sun beside a police box. But when at home, he would always bark at any suspicious person. Among these, the one who received his most furious attack was a ten year old boy from Honjo, a lion-mask dancer. This boy, when he came in, would always say, "Today is a festival day," and would decide not to leave until he had received from the people of the house a crust of bread and a copper. And so, however much Hector barked at him, he would stand his ground. On the contrary, it was Hector who got in the habit of retreating toward the barn, howling, and with his tail between his legs. In short, Hector was a coward, and judged from his behavior he was so degenerated as to be no better than a stray cur. But even so, he never lost the affection for man which is common to his kind. At our frequent meetings he would always wag his tail and jump up at me, or he would unhesitatingly rub his back against me. I don't know how many times he has soiled my clothes and overcoat thus with his muddy paws.

As I was sick last summer until on into the fall, a month elapsed without my being able to see Hector. When my illness became less severe and I was able to leave my bed, I happened to be standing for the first time on the verandah of the tea room, and recognized his figure in the dusk. I promptly called him; but however much I called, he made no response to my advances, but sat motionless beneath the hedge. He did not stir head or tail, but remained like a white lump fixed to the hedge. I could not help but feel a strange kind of sadness, to think that during the separation of a brief month he had forgotten his master's voice.

It was still early fall. The rain doors were not yet closed, and bright starlight could be clearly seen from within the open house. Two or three others were standing with me on the tea room verandah, but they did not even turn to look, when I called Hector. Just as Hector had forgotten me, they too seemed to me to have completely forgotten him.

I returned to my room in silence, and lay down upon the bed spread there. In my convalescence I was wearing a silk garment, trimmed with black silk neck band, hardly suitable for this season. As it was too troublesome to change it, I lay down just as I was, and folding my hands on my breast, silently lay gazing up at the ceiling.

V

The next morning, while standing on my study verandah, casting my eye over the early autumn garden, I accidentally noticed his white form upon the moss. Not wishing to repeat the disappointment of the previous evening I purposely restrained myself from calling his name. But I stood there with my gaze fixed upon him. His head was thrust into a stone basin set at the foot of a tree, and he was lapping up the rain water that was standing in it.

When or by whom this basin was brought in I have no knowledge. When we moved in, it was lying in a corner of the rear yard, and I had the gardener move it to its present position. Its shape was hexagonal, and the entire surface was so covered with moss that it was impossible to read the letters which had been carved on its side. But I remember once, before I had moved there, having read them. And the memory that remains with me is not of the letters, but is of the strange feeling, which even now comes back to me. There was an atmosphere of mutability, such as gathers about a temple or a Buddha.

Hector had his back turned toward me, his tail drooping lifelessly. When he left the basin, I noticed the slaver dripping from his mouth.

"Hector will have to be looked after, for he is ill," I said to my nurse. (At that time I was still under a nurse's care.)

The next day I caught a glimpse of him sleeping among the rushes, and I repeated the same words to my nurse. But Hector from that time on kept himself out of sight, and did not return to the house.

"We intend to take him to the doctor's, but have searched in vain to find him." So said some of my people, watching my face. But I made no reply. However, it aroused in me the memory of what occurred when we first received him. There came back to me the slightly humorous memory of how, when I registered him, under the heading, Species, I wrote, "Mixed"; and under Color, "Red-spotted".

About a week, I should say it was, after he had disappeared, a maid servant came with a message from a house a furlong or two distant from us. She came to tell us that the body of a dog had been found floating on the pond in their garden, and when it had been drawn out, they had found our family name engraved on its collar. The servant inquired whether they should bury the body for us. I immediately sent a rikisha man to go and get it.

I did not know where the house was from which the servant had kindly been sent, but I guessed it might be the house by the old temple which I had known from childhood. That was the temple where was to be found the grave of Yamaga Soko, and just this side of the temple gate was an old Chinese nettle-tree, a reminder of the feudal age, and which could easily be seen, beyond many roofs, from the north verandah of my study.

The rikisha man wrapped the body in straw matting and brought it home. I purposely avoided going near it. I had bought a little white tablet, on which I wrote this line, "I buried him in the earth where autumn winds will never disturb him." I gave this to one of the family to place over the spot where Hector lay. His grave is about six feet northeast of that of our cat. When I step out, from within my glass doors, upon my cool shady north veran-dah, and look out upon the frost-bound rear garden, I can easily see them both. Compared with the dark and decaying tablet above the cat, that of Hector stands out fresh and gleaming. But before long, I imagine, both of them, equally aging, will equally cease to attract our notice.

VI

I met her altogether four or five times. The first time she called I was out. The one who received her at the door told her to bring a letter of introduction with her, but I heard that she left, saying that she had no place to go for such a thing.

A day or so later she wrote me directly, and asked when it would be convenient for me to receive her. From the address on the envelope it appeared that she lived just close by. I returned an immediate answer, appointing a time for her to come.

She came at the time appointed. She was wearing a bright colored silk crepe *haori*, with a crest of three oak leaves, which attracted my attention. She seemed to have read nearly all of my writings, and our conversation drifted chiefly in that direction. But to have one's work praised by a new acquaintance is rather more tickling than pleasing. And to tell the truth, I shrank from being praised.

A week later she called on me again. She spoke in high terms of my writings. But my mind was inclined to avoid such topics of conversation. On the third visit she seemed for some reason to be deeply moved, and kept taking her handkerchief from her sleeve and wiping her tears. She asked me whether I would write the sad story of her life. But not as yet having heard the story I could give her no answer. I asked her whether, in case I should write it, it would cause embarrassment to anyone. She answered in an unusually clear voice that if no names were given there would be no trouble. So, anyhow, I made an appointment with her to hear her life story.

Then when that day came she brought another girl who wished to meet me, and she asked me to postpone the story until her next visit. I had no disposition to blame her for breaking the engagement. We spent the time chatting about the affairs of the day.

On the following evening she sat in my study for the last time. Toying with the brass tongs in the ash-filled brazier before her, and before beginning to tell the sad story of her life, she thus spoke to me, sitting there in silence:

"The other day in my excitement I asked you to kindly write my story, but now I withdraw the request, and ask you merely to listen as I tell it to you. Please let it be that way ..."

To this I replied: "Whatever circumstances may occur to make me wish to write it, you may be assured that I will write nothing at all without your permission."

As I had given her sufficient assurance, she said, "agreed", and began the story of her life from seven or eight years back. I remained in silent gaze upon her face. She kept her eyes downcast, gazing into the brazier. She held the brass tongs in her delicate hands, and kept sticking them into the ashes. Now and then when something unintelligible came out, I would interpose a brief question. She answered simply and satisfactorily to my understanding. But most of the time she did all the talking, sitting as still as a wooden image.

By and by her cheeks flushed red. It was perhaps because she used no powder, but the color of her flushed cheeks especially caught my eye. As she was leaning over, also, her wealth of black hair attracted my attention.

VII

Her confession was so pathetic that my breathing became labored as I listened to it. And then she asked me this question:

"If you were writing such a novel, how would you end this woman's story ?"

I was at a loss for an answer.

"Do you think it were better for her to die, or would you let her live on ?"

I said to her that I might write it either way. And I studied her expression. She seemed to be wanting a more definite answer from me, so knowing no other way, I said to her:

"If you think that to live is the most important thing, you may leave her just as she is; but if you take beauty or nobility as the first principle in the standard of values for humanity, then the question may become quite different."

"But which do you choose ?"

Again I hesitated. I could do nothing but silently listen to what she would say.

"I dread to think that the ravages of time will gradually cause my present precious feeling to fade away. And I shudder with horror when I think of my future, living on, a mere aimless shell, bereft of its soul."

I knew that she was all alone in the world, and immovably held in the iron grip of circumstance. I knew also that her social conditions were such that I had no power to help her. I was placed in the position of a spectator of one whose sufferings I could not reach out my hand to aid.

I had a habit of keeping my watch beside my cushion, even when visitors were present, in order to tell the time for taking my medicine.

"It is already eleven; hadn't you better go?" I finally said to her. She arose without any sign of offense. Then I said to her, "As it is late, may I escort you?" I went down the steps with her.

At that time the beautiful moon was flooding the quiet night with its brightness. When we came out to the road, even our clogs made no sound upon the soft still ground. I followed her, my hands in my pockets and my head bare. At the corner she spoke to me, saying, "It is too much for me to have you escort me." To this I replied, "There is no such thing as 'too much', for we are all alike humans."

When we came to the next corner, again she said, "It is too great an honor to have you see me home."

I asked her seriously, "Do you think it an honor?" to which she answered briefly but clearly, "I do." Then I said, "If so, then you had better live, and not die." I did not know how she would interpret these words. I went a block further on with her, and then turned back toward home.

Having heard her sad and heart-breaking story, I experienced once again a human and wholesome feeling. I experienced the same feeling that one would have after reading a noble piece of literature. I was ashamed to think of how often in the past I had been proud to attend the Euraku or the Imperial Theatre.

VIII

While I tread this thorny path of life, I am always thinking of the realm of death which sooner or later I must reach. I believe, too, that death is easier than life, and I sometimes even think that it is the supreme state of our attainment.

"Death is nobler than life." These words have of late been continually coming and going in my mind.

But my present self is still existing. Not being able to transcend in my one life the habits formed by my parents, grandparents, great-grandparents, through a period of a hundred, two hundred, a thousand, ten thousand years, I am still clinging to this life. So that I feel that my advice to others must be within the bounds of this life. I feel that I, as one man, must face other men only within the narrow limits of our way of living. For it is our proper understanding to base our fundamental principles upon this life, however painful and ugly it may be, since I recognize myself as acting within this life, and recognize others as living within their own sphere of life.

"If life is so hard, it were better to die." Such words as these would not be heard even from the one who finds the world most unkind. The physician, for example, by means of the hypodermic needle, contrives to prolong, even for a moment, the life of the patient who is on the very verge of his eternal sleep. When we realize how this device, so akin to torture, is regarded as a blessing to mankind, we can readily understand how tenaciously we cling to life. Therefore I could not urge her to choose death rather than life.

She had been so deeply wounded in heart that her recovery seemed hopeless. At the same time this wound became the source of sweet memories, beyond the experience of ordinary mortals, and brought a light into her face.

She wished to keep this beautiful thing, like a jewel, safe forever in her inmost heart. But unfortunately the beautiful thing was none other than the wound itself, which had been tormenting her more cruelly than death. The two were no more separable than the two sides of a sheet of paper.

I told her to go down along the stream of Time which is all healing. But she lamented that, if so, this precious memory would be gradually lost.

Impartial Time, while robbing her of her precious jewel, will gradually heal the wound of her heart. While it may bedim, like a dream, the intense joys of life, still it never fails to remove the fresh pain which accompanies present joys.

So I let Time wipe away the bleeding drops from her wound, though it might also remove the passionate memory deeply rooted in her intense love. However commonplace life may be, it seemed to me more proper for her to live than to die.

Thus, though I always believed death to be nobler than life, my hope and and advice for her could not finally go beyond this life, so filled with unhappiness. And this simply proved, from the practical point of view, that I was no better than an ordinary follower of naturalism. To this day I look into my inmost heart half-distrustfully.

IX

Among my comparatively intimate friends in High School days there was a Mr. O. I, who have subsequently formed but few friendships, was naturally inclined to have frequent visits with him. I called on him an average of once a week, and during one summer vacation called on him at his boarding house at Masago Cho, every day without fail, and induced him to go with me to the swimming place on the Sumida River.

As O. was from the north, he had the characteristic manner of speech, gentle and slow, very different from my own. And that manner of speech seemed to fitly express his disposition. Though I remember having had many arguments with him, I have never seen his face angry or excited. For that fact alone, I considered him fully worthy of respect, and recognized him as my superior.

As his disposition was more generous, so was his intellect far greater than my own. He was often thinking out for himself problems far beyond my ability to grasp. While he had, from the beginning, intended to enter the science course, he enjoyed reading philosophical books. I still remember having once borrowed from him Spencer's First Principles.

On fine clear autumn days we often walked whithersoever our footsteps led us, conversing with each other. On such occasions we would often observe such scenes as the falling of the little yellow-tinged leaves from the branches of trees, extending from behind the fences out over the road, even though no wind was blowing. And when this suddenly caught his eye he would exclaim in a low voice, "Ah! I understand." To me, who could see only the beauty of the floating colors on the autumn sky, his words produced only strange echoes, like the symbol of mystic spirits. Afterwards he would explain in his usual slow way, as if talking to himself, "Understanding is a wonderful thing." I had no word to say in reply.

He was a student of limited means. While boarding himself in a rented room near the Kwannon Temple, he often invited me to a frugal meal of broiled salt salmon. Sometimes instead of rice cakes he bought boiled beans, and we enjoyed eating them with chopsticks from the bamboo leaves in which they had been wrapped.

Not long after graduating from the university he went to his post in a country Middle School. I felt very sorry for him for that. But to his university professors, who did not really know him, that may have seemed quite proper. He accepted it, of course, with equanimity. After some years he went to China, if I remember correctly, on a three year contract as a school teacher. After completing his term he came back, and immediately became principal of a Middle School in the country. Even then he was transferred from Akita to Yokote, and at present he is a school principal in Saghalien.

When, for the first time in years he visited Tokyo and called on me, I, receiving his card from the attendant, and without waiting for the visitor to first enter, immediately went into the guest room, and sat down awaiting his coming. He had no sooner seen me sitting properly on the floor cushion than he said, "You are putting on airs, eh?"

Before he had finished his words, "Yes" slipped unintentionally from my lips. Why such an answer, which confirmed his abuse of me, should so naturally and easily and smoothly have escaped my tongue, I knew not. At that time I had a feeling of high exaltation.

X

When O. and I sat down opposite each other, first of all we looked into each other's face, and saw still the traces of our old features, lingering on like faint memories of sweet dreams. But just as an old heart becomes interwoven in new moods, so they likewise seemed enveloped in a light haze. For neither of us was it possible, resisting the dread force of Time, to return once more to the old forms. We could not help looking back upon the strange past that had intervened since we had separated.

In the old days O. had had cheeks as red as apples, unusually large round eyes, and a face as round and smooth as a woman's. Now, too, he seemed to have the same red cheeks, round eyes, the same rounded outline of face; yet someway he looked different from of old.

I showed him my moustache and side hair, and he in turn stroked the top of his head. Mine was gettng white; his was getting thin.

"Having gone as far as Saghalien, you couldn't go any farther, could you?" I asked, banteringly. To this he replied,"Very likely not". He then told me many strange stories about Saghalien. However, I have forgotten them all by now. I only remember that Saghalien is a delightful place in summer.

For the first time in many years we went out together. He was wearing a loose mantled overcoat over his frock coat. While hanging to a strap in the electric car, he drew from his pocket something wrapped in a handkerchief, and showed it to me. I asked him what it was, and he replied that it was some chestnut cakes. These were the cakes which just a little while ago I had served him in my home. I was a bit surprised to think that he had wrapped them up in a handkerchief this way.

"Have you brought those chestnut cakes along?"

"I shouldn't be surprised." He spoke as if he were making fun of my surprise, and put the handkerchief parcel into his pocket.

That evening we went to the Imperial Theatre. My two tickets indicated the north entrance, but I was carelessly about to go around to the south entrance when he cautioned me, "Not that way." I paused to think for a moment, and then turned back to the proper entrance with the remark, "I see that Saghalien is right as far as the direction is concerned."

He told me that he had known the Imperial Theatre from the beginning. But after we had finished our supper, and were about to return to our seats, like all the rest, he mistook the second floor door for the first, and then it was my turn to laugh.

Now and then he took his gold-rimmed glasses from his pocket and read some printed matter that was in his hand, then calmly looked at the distant stage without removing them.

"Aren't those reading glasses ? How can you see things at a distance with them ?"

"Why, they are *chabudo*."

I didn't know at all the meaning of this *chabudo*; but he explained that it was a Chinese word meaning "all the same."

On the way home that night we separated in the street car. He went back to that cold far-northern frontier of our Japanese territory.

Whenever I recall him, I think of the name Master, and I feel as if that name were specially given by Heaven for him. And I think of the Master as still a Middle School principal in that far north land, bound in with ice and snow.

A certain lady introduced a girl to me. "She says she wishes you to look at something she has written."

These words of the lady brought to my mind a number of things. Hitherto any number of people had come asking me to read what they themselves had written. Among these manuscripts some have been one or two inches in thickness, but I have read them through, as far as time has permitted. I was simple enough to be satisfied with the feeling that I had fulfilled the duty imposed upon me, by merely reading them. However, these people nearly always asked me afterwards to please publish it for them in a paper or magazine. Among these there were not a few whose real motive in having me read it seemed to be to exchange the manuscript for cash. It gradually became distasteful to me to read, out of pure kindness, illegible manuscripts written by total strangers.

Of course, it is true that I had more time at my disposal than when I was a teacher. But even so, when I attended to my own business, my mind was fully occupied. And it sometimes happened that I made almost no headway even with the manuscripts which, out of kindness, I had promised to read.

I told the lady the very thoughts that were in my mind. She fully understood my meaning and left. It was soon afterwards that the expected girl came to my room and sat down upon the floor cushion. Gazing through the glass door at the leaden sky, from which a gloomy rain seemed about to fall, I spoke thus to her: —

"This is not a social affair. We cannot expect to get anywhere or gain anything, however long we may continue, while we merely address each other in polite phrases and forms. You must bring yourself to be absolutely frank with me. If you will, on your part, frankly reveal yourself to me, I shall be able to see clearly the true facts as to where you stand, and whither you are facing. Then only shall I be conscious of having received from you due qualifications as to directing you. Therefore, when I say anything, and you have something in your mind to reply, you must by no means remain silent. For if you refrain, fearing that you will be laughed at for something you might say, or be ashamed, or scolded for some discourtesy, and try to show me only that part of you that is disguised, however hard I may try to give you help, my arrows will certainly fail to hit the mark.

"This is what I request of you. And I, on my part, will not conceal my true self from you. There is no other way to teach you but to expose things just as they are. So if there is somewhere in my thoughts an opening that you can take advantage of, the result as far as I am concerned will be failure, in the sense that you have found my weak point. It is a mistake to think that only the one who receives the teaching has the duty of exposing himself.

The one who teaches also must open himself up before you. Both of us together, setting aside all social amenities, must look clearly into each other.

"For this reason, when I hereafter look at your writings, I may perhaps have to say quite severe things, but you must not be angry. For I do not say them intending to hurt your feelings. And you, on your part, if there are things you do not understand, please attack me as much as you wish. In so far as you understand my intentions, I shall certainly have no reason to be angry.

"In a word, this is an entirely different matter from a social affair, whose chief function is polished smoothness, with the purpose of preserving the status quo. Is this clear to you?"

She said that she understood, and went away.

People sometimes ask me to autograph a poem on the customary paper strip, or some other verses. And they send me the paper strip or piece of silk to write on, even before I have given my consent. At first, not wishing to disappoint their expressed desire, though my hand writing is poor enough, I wrote as they requested. But finding it hard to continue these favors indefinitely, my tendency to ignore these requests of many people became stronger and stronger. As I sometimes even think that all men are born for daily shame, I might possibly send my poor handwriting, if I cared to do so. But when ill or busy, or when I did not feel like doing such a thing, as the demand kept coming, I proved unequal to the task. Most of these people were utter strangers to me, and seemed to give no consideration at all to the trouble it gave me to return these strips which they had sent me.

Among these, the one that displeased me most was a man named Iwasaki, who lived at Sagoshi in the Province of Banshu. This is the man whom I remember as having, some years before, often requested me by post card to write a haiku for him, and whose request I had regularly complied with. Some years later he sent me a thin square parcel. I thought it too much trouble even to open it, so left it there in the study, just as it was; and when the servant cleaned the room, she stuck it in between my books, so that it looked as if it were properly put away.

About the same time as this parcel there came to me from Nagoya a can of tea. I had no idea as to its sender or its purpose. I drank the tea without any hesitation. Immediately thereafter there came from the man of Sagoshi a request that I send back to him the picture of climbing Mt. Fuji. As I had no recollection of having received any such thing from him, I paid no heed to it. But he kept on urging me to send back the picture. I finally began to have suspicions of his mental state. "Perhaps he is crazy," I said to myself, and paid no attention to his insistence.

Two or three months passed by. It was about the beginning of summer, as I recall. I was weary of sitting in my study with things scattered about in such confusion, so began to put things by myself in order, here and there. When, in order to arrange my books properly I was going, volume by volume, over the dictionaries and reference books that stood in careless piles, I unexpectedly came across that parcel which the man of Sagoshi had sent me. With surprise I saw before my eyes that which I had altogether forgotten. When I broke the seal and looked within, I discovered a small folded picture, and was again surprised when it proved to be a picture of the ascent of Mt. Fuji.

There was also in the parcel, in addition to the picture, a letter asking me to autograph the picture with some comment, stating also that he was sending me some tea by way of thanks. I was still more surprised.

But I had then no courage at all to write any comment on the Fuji climbing picture. My mood was far removed from anything of that sort, and I was not disposed to think of a poem appropriate to the picture. But I was filled with regret, and wrote a courteous letter of apology for my negligence. I also expressed my thanks for the tea. And last of all I wrapped up the picture and sent it back.

XIII

Thinking that I had made an end of it, I gave no further thought to the affair of this Sagoshi man. Then he himself sent me a letter enclosing a *tanzaku* or paper strip, and asked me this time to write a verse about the Loyal Samurai. I replied that I would at some time do so. But no opportunity presenting itself, I left it undone. This pestilential fellow, however, had no intentions of leaving things as they were, and began to pester me ceaselessly. His demand was sure to come every week or every other week. It was always in the form of a postcard, and always began with the words, "Dear sir, I am sorry to trouble you, but ..." I gradually came to dislike the very sight of the postcards.

At the same time his urgency came to take on such strange characteristics as I had hardly anticipated. At first there appeared such words as, "Did I not send you some tea?" When I paid no attention to that, he changed his tune to, "Please send me back the tea." I wanted to send him word that, though it was easy enough to send it, I didn't care to take the trouble, and if he wished to come to Tokyo and get it, I would hand it over to him. But realizing that it would bemean myself to write such a letter to the man of Sagoshi, I dared not bring myself to do it. And yet he, receiving no answer, dunned me more than ever. He said that it was alright for me not to return the tea, but to please remit to him its value, one yen. My feelings toward this fellow gradually grew ruffled. I finally forgot myself entirely. I wrote him that I had drunk the tea, lost the strip, and it would be absolutely useless for him to send any more post cards. Then I experienced an exceedingly bitter feeling in my heart. For I thought that this Sagoshi man had driven me into the situation where I must make such an ungentlemanly reply. I felt badly to think that I had to suffer even the slightest injury to my character or personality on account of this fellow.

But the man of Sagoshi was unperturbed. He wrote me another card, saying, "To have drunk the tea and lost the strip is too much ..." But at the beginning, as before, was written the identical words, "Dear sir, I am sorry to trouble you, but ..."

I thereupon determined to have no further dealings with this fellow. But of course my determination had no effect upon his attitude toward me. He kept on with his demands. Now he wrote, "If you will write once more I will send you some more tea. How about it?" Then, "Since from the nature of the case it concerns the Loyal Samurai, you might as well compose a verse."

Then when I thought the postcards had stopped for a time, they changed to letters. The envelope was very cheap and gray, such as is used at the Ward Office. But he purposely failed to attach a stamp to it. And in addition, he had posted it without writing his name on the back. On that account I had to pay double the postage, twice over. At last I gave his name and address to the postman, and had him send it back unopened. And so, perhaps as the result of having to pay six sen, he seemed finally to have ceased his demands.

It happened that two years later, when the new year came in, he sent me an ordinary card of greeting. It was a bit gratifying, so I decided to write a verse on a paper strip and send it to him. But this gift was not enough to satisfy him. He ceaselessly demanded that I should write it over, on the plea that this one was torn or soiled. Only this January, on the seventh or eighth, there came to me a request, "I am sorry to trouble you, but ...."

I had never before in my life run across such a man as this.

XIV

I have only recently heard the details of how, a long time ago, robbers entered our home. As to when it happened, since it was when neither of my elder sisters had yet married, it must have been about the time I was born. At any rate it was during the boisterous period when such rough words as royalists and feudalists were in common use.

One night, when my eldest sister had to get up, she opened the little side door in order to wash her hands, and saw a flash of light in the corner of the little inner garden, where the trunk of an old plum tree stood forcefully, as if pressing back the wall. Before having time to give it thought, she quickly closed the door; but after closing it, while standing there, she considered the strange light which she had just seen before her.

The face of this eldest sister was so imprinted in my childish memory that even now, when I would recall it, it stands out clearly before my mind's eye. But that is a picture of her after she had married and had her teeth blackened; so it is a bit hard for me to picture her in my mind as a blooming maiden, standing there at that time thoughtfully, upon the verandah.

Broad forehead, darkish skin, small, but clearly outlined nose, double-lidded eyes, larger than the ordinary, and the gentle name of O-Sawa—putting all these together, I can just imagine how my sister looked on this occasion.

While she stood there thinking for a time, it came to her that it might have been a fire. At the moment that she had decided to open the door again and was about to peep out, there appeared out of the darkness, through the square aperture in the little side door, a gleaming sword. She drew back in amazement. They say that meanwhile the burglars, with masked faces, carrying dark lanterns and with swords unsheathed, came by the little side door into the house where we all were. I was told that there were eight of the robbers in all. They said that they had not come to kill anyone, and that if all kept quiet they would do no harm to anyone in the house; but then father must give them money for the army, they said. Father protested that he had none, but the burglars would by no means be convinced. They were immovable, saying that they had just entered the wine shop of Oguraya on the corner, and had got their information there, so that it would be useless to try to conceal it. My father then, with great reluctance spread before them some *koban* (gold coins). Perhaps it was because they thought the amount of money was too small; they would not leave. So my mother who had until now been lying in bed, urged him to give them all the money that was in his purse. The story goes that there was something like fifty yen. After the robbers had left they say that father scolded mother, saying, "You women talk too much".

After this had occurred, our family devised the plan of hollowing out a pillar and hiding money inside it; but we never made money enough to hide, nor did any masked burglars ever come again, so that when I grew up I could never even tell which pillar had been hollowed out.

When the burglars went away, they complimented us on having a well secured house. But from that day on, the head of Hambei San of Oguraya, who had told the burglars of that well-secured house, bore the scars of many wounds. It is said that every time he assured the burglars that there was no money there, they, declaring that this could not be true, had pricked Hambei's head slightly with the point of a drawn sword. But even so he kept on saying, "There isn't any in the house at all. Natsume San in the rear has plenty. Why don't you go there?" So at last he came through without having lost a penny.

I got this story from my wife, who in turn had heard it over the tea cups from my elder brother.

XV

I delivered a lecture at the Peers' School last November, and later a paper parcel was delivered at my house, with the words, "In Token of Gratitude" written upon it. It was tied with ceremonial cord, and when I untied it and looked inside, I found there two five yen bills. Thinking to give it to a certain artist friend of mine, for whom I was always feeling sympathy, I quietly awaited his coming. However, before the artist made his appearance, occasion arose for making a contribution to something or other, so I disposed of the two bills.

To say in a word, this money, as far as I was concerned, was by no means uselessly spent. I cannot deny that according to the world standard it was well expended on myself. Viewed from my subjective intention to give it to someone else, it was without doubt money with no gratitude attached. To speak frankly, I feel far better not to receive such a token of gratitude. In the course of a conversation I had with Mr. Kaishu Kuroyanagi when he came to see me in regard to a lecture at the Chogyu Meeting, I told him fully my reasons.

"In this case I didn't go to sell my energies. I simply complied with their request out of kindness; and I think that they too should repay me with goodwill alone. If they had intended to make it a matter of payment, they should from the first have consulted as to whether or not I would come for a certain fee."

Mr. K. looked as if he could not clearly understand me, and replied.

"But see here. Why not regard that ten yen as meaning not the purchase of your efforts, but a method of expressing to you their feeling of gratitude ?"

"I could very easily interpret it that way if it were in the form of some article, but unfortunately their thanks took the form of money, which is used in ordinary mercantile exchange, in buying and selling, so that we could look at it either way."

"Well, if you could take it either way, isn't it proper to interpret it in the better way?"

That seemed reasonable enough. But again I replied "As you know, I just about support myself with my pen. Of course I could not be called rich. By hook or crook I have managed to get through each day as it came. Therefore, in matters outside my own vocation, I desire, out of kindness, to do as much as possible for others. And so, for that kindness to be accepted by them is to me the highest reward of all. Therefore, when I receive such a thing as money the margin left me for working in behalf of others —a margin which today is for me exceedingly narrow — I feel as if this precious margin were being encroached upon."

Mr. K. still seemed not to agree with what I said, but I also held my ground.

"Supposing you should ask such wealthy people as Iwasaki or Mitsui to give a lecture, would you afterwards take them a ten yen fee? Or, thinking that to be discourteous, would you let it be sufficient to merely express your gratitude in words ? It is my opinion that you would probably not take cash to them."

"Well," was all that Mr. K. would say, not offering a more definite reply. But I had something more that I wished to say.

"I may be conceited, but, even though I am not rich as compared with Mitsui or Iwasaki, I feel certain that I am far richer than the general run of students."

"That's so." And Mr. K. nodded in agreement.

"If it is discourteous to take a ten yen fee to Iwasaki or Mitsui, it is equally discourteous to bring it to me. In case that ten yen were to give great relief to my material welfare I might look at the question from a different view point. But, as a matter of fact, I intended to give it away, for in my present economic condition ten yen would mean practically nothing at all to me."

"I will think it over," said Mr. K., and left, with a smile on his face.

XVI

Down a gentle slope in front of my house there stands a bridge, crossing a little six-foot stream. Just beyond it, on the left-hand side stands a little barber shop. I have had my hair cut there just once.

Its interior, behind the glass doors, was usually concealed from the view of the street by a gingham curtain, so that until I had entered the shop and seated myself before the mirror, I had no idea what the barber looked like.

When he saw me enter, he threw down the newspaper he was holding in his hand, and made a bow. I then felt an inescapable impression that this was certainly a man whom I had met somewhere. Then when he went around behind me and started clipping with his scissors, I took the opportunity to open a conversation with him. I learned that, as I had guessed, he had long ago kept a shop beside the Post Office in Tera Machi, making his living then as now by plying his scissors.

"I received many favors from Mr. Takada." This Takada being my cousin, I was taken by surprise, and said,

"What! Do you know Takada? "

"Know him? I should say so. He always patronized me, and called me by my first name."

His use of language was rather polite for an artisan.

When I told him that Takada was not now living, he lifted his voice in an exclamation of surprise.

"Oh, that's too bad. He was a fine man. When did he pass away?"

"Why, very recently. Just about two weeks or so ago."

He then told me various things that he remembered of this deceased cousin of mine, closing with the words, "How quickly, sir, time passes when we look back. While it seems but a matter of a day ago, almost thirty years have already gone by."

"He lived in the little side street of the Kyuyutei." The barber again took up the story.

"Yes, it was that two story house, wasn't it ?"

"Yes, it was that house with the second floor. When he moved into it, he received many congratulatory gifts and had a great time. It was afterwards, wasn't it, that he moved into the temple grounds of the Gyogwanji."

I could not answer this inquiry. As a matter of fact it was an affair of so long ago that I had forgotten it entirely.

"These temple grounds seem now to have greatly changed. I have had no occasion to visit there since then."

"Changed ? I should say so. There is nothing there now but assignation houses."

I knew that whenever I went along Sakana Machi I could see a lot of square lanterns hanging at the entrance of the narrow lane, with a sock store on the corner, as you enter the temple grounds. But I didn't have interest enough to try to count their number, and so had not been aware of what he now told me.

"Sure enough! Now that you speak of it, I remember having seen from the street such signs as, 'The Sleeve.'"

"Yes, many have come there. When we stop to think of it, we ought to expect great changes, for thirty years have already gone by. Speaking of geisha houses, there was, as you know, at that time, but one in the temple grounds. It was the Azumaya. It was just opposite Mr. Takada's that the lantern of the Azumaya was hung out."

XVII

I remembered that Azumaya quite well. As it was just across from my cousin's house, they were well enough acquainted to merely bow to each other if they happened to meet, whenever they went in or out.

My second eldest brother, at that time, was whiling away his time at my cousin's house. This brother of mine was a great profligate, and had a bad habit of frequently stealing scrolls and swords from the house, and disposing of them for little or nothing. At the time I did not know why he had been bundled over into my cousin's house, but when I now think of it, I imagine it was because of some such outrage that he was for a time expelled from our home. Besides this elder brother there was a fellow named Sho San, who also was a cousin on my mother's side, idling his time away there.

These fellows would always be together, lying around, or sitting on the verandah, talking about nothing in particular. They were sometimes hailed from the lattice window of the geisha house across the way by a voice calling, "Good day." And, as if they had been awaiting it, these fellows would call the girls over, with some such words as, "Say, come over a minute. We have something for you." As the geisha girls, on their part, had liberty in the daytime, they came over, out of friendliness, about once in three times. That was the general trend of things.

I was then seventeen or eighteen, and moreover passed for an exceedingly shy lad, so if I happened to be in such a place, I would have nothing at all to say, but would keep myself hidden away in a corner. Even so, by some strange chance I went with these fellows to the geisha house to play, and had a game of cards. As the one who lost had to treat the others, I ate a great many rice balls and cakes that others had to pay for.

About a week later I was again taken by this idle brother of mine to the same house, to play, and finding Sho San seated there, carried on with him a lively conversation. A young girl, named Sakimatsu, seeing me, said, "Let's have another game of cards." I was wearing wide trousrs (*hakama*) of duck cloth, and sitting there stiffly. But I didn't have a penny of change in my purse.

"I don't want to, for I haven't a cent."

"Never mind. I have."

She must have had some eye trouble at the time, and while speaking, she kept rubbing her slightly-inflamed double eyelids with the sleeve of her pretty underwaist.

Later on I heard it said at my cousin's house that O-Saku had been taken away by a wealthy patron. At my cousin's house they spoke of this girl not as Sakimatsu, but always, O-Saku, they called her. When I heard this report, I thought within my heart that I should never have a chance to meet O-Saku again.

It happened long afterwards that, when I went with that Master to the Sannai Bazaar in Shiba, I met O-Saku there face to face. I still appeared in student style, but she had been transformed into a respectable matron. One who appeared to be her husband was beside her.

This incident alone suddenly came to mind out of the hidden depths of the name, Azumaya Geisha House, when spoken by the lips of the barber.

"Do you know the girl called O-Saku who lived there?" I asked him.

"Know her ? Why, she is my niece."

"Is that so ?" I was amazed.

"Well, where is she now ?"

"O-Saku has died, sir." Again I was amazed.

"When?"

"When? It is now long ago. I think it was in her twenty third year."

"Ah !"

"Yes, and it was at Vladivostok that she died. Her husband was in the Consulate there, and she went with him. It was almost immediately afterwards that she died."

After going home, and sitting down within my glass doors, I felt as if the only ones not yet dead were myself and the barber.

XVIII

A certain young lady was ushered into my parlor, and said to me, "I am perplexed because everything about me is awry. I don't know what to do."

As she was living in the home of some relative, I supposed that the house was not large enough, and that she was disturbed by the children, so my reply to her was quite brief.

"Why don't you search for a quieter house, and take lodging there ?"

"No, it isn't a matter of room. It is my mind that is awry. That is what worries me."

I was conscious of having misunderstood her, but at the same time I again failed to make out what she could mean. So I asked her to go on further in explanation.

"Anything from without can get into my head alright, but it will not harmonize with my mind's center."

"What is it that you mean by your 'mind's center'?"

"What do I mean? I mean a straight line."

I knew that she was greatly interested in mathematics, but what she meant by the mind's center being a straight line was naturally beyond me. Moreover, I could hardly understand what she meant by the expression, the mind's center. She went on.

"Everything has a center, hasn't it?"

"That's true of material things which the eye can see

and the rule can measure. But does the mind have form? If so, please show me what you call its center."

The girl, without saying whether she would show it to me or not, now looked out toward the garden, now rubbed her knees with her two hands.

"What you call a straight line is a figure of speech, isn't it? If so, doesn't it come to the same thing whether it is round or square?"

"Perhaps so, but there really is something which never changes at all, among these things which are always changing their color and form."

"If what is changeable and what is unchangeable are different, then you have two separate minds. Wouldn't that be so? Isn't it unescapable, then, that the changeable must be unchangeable?"

So saying, I came back to the original question with the girl.

"I suppose there is no one who, when external things enter his mind, can dispose of them neatly, orderly and in their proper relations. Pardon me if I suggest that, with your years, your education and learning, you would hardly be expected to harmonize them. If this does not express your meaning, and if you wish to thoroughly harmonize and dispose of everything without the aid of learning, then it is useless to come to such a person as myself. You had better go to a priest."

At this she looked me in the face.

"When I first saw you, I felt that your mind, at this point, was better ordered than that of most men."

"No, that cannot be so."

"Anyhow, it seemed so to me. I could not help thinking that even the location of your internal organs must be harmonious."

"If my internal organs were so harmoniously regulated, I should not always be sick like this."

"I am never sick," she said suddenly, referring to herself.

"That shows that you are superior to me, " I answered.

She slipped from the cushion, and retired from the room, with the words, "Please take good care of your health."

XIX

My old home was in a place called Baba-Shita, four or five blocks from where I now live. Though it was called a town, the fact was that it was hardly more than a travelers' stopping place, and in my childhood days seemed deserted and lonely. Originally what was called Baba-Shita meant the spot below Takata-no-Baba, and it was certainly in such an out-of-the-way corner that when we look at the Views of Yedo we cannot tell whether it is within the limits or not.

But even so there were three or four houses in the little town that were built in store house style. One of these was the drug store of Dembei Omiya, to be seen on the right hand side as you go up the slope. Then just at the foot of the slope was a wine shop with its wide entrance, called the Kokuraya. Though this was not of storehouse construction, it was a house that preserved the history of how Yasubei Horibe, when he took revenge upon his enemy at Takada-no-Baba, had stopped here and drunk a great measure of wine. I had known the story from childhood, but never saw the measure which Yasubei held to his lips, and which was rumored to have been kept there. But instead of that I often heard the *Naga-uta* sung by his daughter O-Kita San. As I was but a child I could not tell whether she was a good singer or not. But while standing on the stones that led from the verandah to the front gate, as I was about to go out to the street, I could easily hear O-Kita San's voice. On a spring afternoon I would stand, leaning dreamily against the white wall of our store-house, bathing my enchanted soul in the bright sunshine, and half listening to O-Kita San's music. That is how I came all unconsciously to learn such lines as, *"Tabi no koromo wa suzu-gake no."*

Besides these there was a pole-maker's, and there was also a blacksmith shop. There was also a vegetable market, a wide earthen place enclosed beneath a roof, a little distance in the direction of Hachiman-zaka. Our folks called its owner Santaro San, the wholesale dealer. I heard something about Santaro San's being a distant relative of my father, but to speak of intimacy, that was altogether lacking. It seemed to me that they had no more relation with each other than to make a conventional reference to the weather when they passed on the street. This Santaro's only daughter fell in love with a story-teller known as Teisui, and I remember its having been said that there was much ado over their making it a matter of life and death; but I have no definite memory of it any more. To me, as a child, far more interesting to behold was the scene of Santaro San, sitting on a high stool, with his ink brush and account book in his hands, shouting in brave tones, "How much am I offered?" and surveying the sea of faces beneath him. And below him twenty or thirty hands were raised at once, and all facing toward Santaro, shouting as if in anger such cryptic words as "Ronji" and "garen", and then quickly carrying away in their muscular arms the baskets of ginger, egg-plants or squashes— all this was a brave sight to see.

There was, of course, the bean-curd seller, which is sure to be found in every country place. A curtain, saturated with the smell of oil hung at the bean-curd shop, and before its entrance there flowed a ditch of water as pure as that of Kyoto. If you should turn at the bean-curd shop, you could see, about half a block ahead, the measurably high temple gate of the Seikanji. Within the red-lacquered gate all was covered by a thick bamboo grove, and what was within it could not be seen at all from the street; but the sound of the bell in the rear, at morning and evening service, even now rings in my ears. More especially, from the misty autumn to the bleak, windy winter, the sound of the Seikanji bell always chilled my boyish spirit, as though it were driving into my heart something sad and cold.

XX

I still remember, as though it were a dream, that there was a story-teller's next door to the bean curd shop. Perhaps it is because one would hardly expect to find a story-teller's in such a remote place that my memory is hazy, and that whenever I call it to mind, I am struck with a strange feeling, and always look back upon my distant past with wide-eyed wonder.

The proprietor of the story-teller's was the fire chief of the ward, and sometimes went out, wearing the black striped apron and the coat with red-lined insignia, and with his sandals slipped on. He had a daughter, too, called O-Fuji San, and I still remember that our folks often spoke about her good looks. She later took a husband into the family, and I was a bit surprised to find him a fine, mustached gentleman. O-Fuji San, too, was popularly said to be proud of her husband; but on later inquiry I was told that he was a clerk in some ward office.

At the time this new member of the family came, the hall was closed and there seemed to be nothing going on. But in former times, when the dark lonely sign was hanging there under the eaves of the house, I used often to get money from my mother and go there to hear the story-telling. If I remember correctly the story-teller's name was Nan-Rin. Strangely enough, no other story-teller than Nan-Rin seemed to have appeared at this house.

I don't know where his house was, but from whatever direction he might have come, it must have required considerable effort, compared with the well-constructed and well-laid-out streets of today. Moreover, since the audience always numbered fifteen or twenty, however much I stretch my imagination, I cannot help feeling that it is all a dream. "At the call, '*Oiran*', Yatsu-hashi made reply, and at that instant the gleam of a sword flashed—" Whether I learned this strange sentence from Nan-Rin at that time, or memorized it later on, in imitation of some professional story-teller, is not now clear in my mind.

In those days, when I would go to some more town-like town, I had to pass through deserted tea fields, bamboo groves, and long paths between the rice paddies. If we bought anything worth buying we usually had to go to Kagura-zaka for it; and to me, accustomed as I was to such necessities, it should not have been such a troublesome journey, but nevertheless, to go up to Yarai-zaka, passing by the fire tower of Sakai Sama, and going on over to Tera Machi, those five or six blocks of straight walking were lonely enough even in day-time, and were always as dark as if the sky were overcast.

Many great trees, with circumference two or three times the length of one's outstretched arms, were there, and the spaces between them were filled with bamboo groves, so that as for a chance to see the sun, there was perhaps not a moment in the day when that was possible.

If, intending to go down town, I started off on my fair weather clogs, I was sure to meet with difficulties. I vividly recall that the thaw there was more terrible than rain or snow.

Even in such an out-of-the-way place there was apparently the fear of fire, and, as you might expect, a high ladder stood at the corner of the street, at its top an old fire bell hanging, true to form. I often recall these old-time things just as they were. There now floats before my eyes the little eating shop which was directly beneath the fire bell. I can never forget the effect of the warm smell of cooking and smoke as they came out together from between the curtains, flooding into the street, and permeating the evening haze. The verse which I wrote while Shiki was still living, "O tall winter trees, beside the fire alarm," was really composed in honor of this fire bell.

XXI

My memories of my home are generally those of such country life. And somehow, a cold, dark, pitiful shadow hovers over it all. So when I quite recently heard from my surviving elder brother the story of how my elder sisters went to the theatre in those days, I was surprised. When I think of there having been an olden time when they lived in such a style, I cannot help, more than ever, feeling that it must be a dream.

In those days the theatres were all in Saru-waka Street. And as there were no electric cars or jinrikisha at that time, it was no easy matter to get there early in the morning, all the way from below Takada-no-Baba to beyond the Kwanron Temple of Asakusa. My sisters all got up at midnight to make their preparations. And to guard against robbers on the way, a man servant seems always to have accompanied them.

They would go down Tsukudo, and from Kakino-Ki side street come out to the landing, then embark in the covered boat which had been ordered in advance at the boat house there. I can imagine how their minds were filled with expectation as they were slowly rowed from in front of the arsenal, past O-Cha-no-Mizu, and as far as the Yanagi Bridge. However, that their journey by no means ended here gives me food for recalling that in the olden days no limit was placed upon time.

They say that after the boat came out into the Great River, it went up stream, passed the Azuma Bridge, and ended its journey at the side of the Yumeiro at Imado. My sisters alighted there, and walked to the theatre tea-house, from which they were directed to the theatre itself, and at length reached the seats reserved for them. These reserved seats were always in the high pit. As this was the place where the occupant's dress, face, hair decorations and other show could easily attract the eye of the whole house, people who were fond of style vied with each other to obtain these seats.

Between the acts the actors' servant would invite the people to come and visit them in their room, and would conduct them there. Then my sisters would follow the man, dressed in *hakama* over his figured silk kimono, into the room of some such favorite actor as Tanosuke or Tossho; later coming back with a fan on which he had drawn a picture for them. This must have been a matter of pride to them. And it could not have been obtained without the power of money.

On their return they were rowed back as far as the landing in the same boat and the same way by which they had come. And the man servant again, for the sake of caution, went to meet them with a lighted lantern. They probably reached home about twelve o'clock, according to present-day reckoning. So they were barely able to see the play by spending the time from midnight to midnight.

When I hear such a spectacular story, I wonder whether such things happened in my own home after all. I feel as if it must be the old-time story of some rich down-town family.

However, our family was not of samurai class. It was the head family of the town, and had to put on style. The father whom I knew was an old man with a bald head, but in his early years he was said to have learned how to sing the Itchu Bushi ballads, and to have presented a set of silk quilts to his lady love. I heard that he had rice fields in Aoyama, and that the produce of these alone would be sufficient to support his family. As a matter of fact, my third elder brother, who is still living, says that he could always hear the sound of the polishing of that rice. It is my recollection that all the people of the town, when they spoke of our house, called it *Genkan, Genkan*. At that time I did not know why, but as I think of it now, I presume it was becsuse it was the only house in the town that had a dignified portico at the entrance. I can still remember the olden days when on going up on the stoop there could be seen hanging there in a row such punitive instruments as whipping rods, sleeve catching spears, and three pronged spears, and old-fashioned horse lanterns.

XXII

For two or three years past I have had an average of one spell of sickness each year. Nearly a month elapsed from the time I was taken down until I was able to leave my bed.

My sickness has always been stomach trouble. When it came to the worst, there was no other method of treatment than abstention from food. Not only the orders of the physician, but the nature of the illness also, forced upon me this course of fasting. And so I am more thin and dizzy when I approach recovery than when the illness begins. It seems to be mostly due to this weakness that the attacks continue for more than a month.

When my movements become more free again, I often find black-bordered cards of announcement lying on my desk. As one who smiles grimly at fate, I put on my silk hat, and taking my place in the funeral procession, ride in a rikisha to the ceremony. Among those who have died there are old men and women, but sometimes there are those of younger years than myself, and even some who could always boast of having good health.

On returning home I sit before my desk and think how truly strange is the span of human life. I wonder why I, who am so often sick, should survive these. Why should these meet an earlier death than I?

It is but natural that I should indulge in such meditations. For the most part I live on, thinking it quite the natural thing that I should not die, as one who is liable to forget everything that constitutes his own self—his position, his body, his talents. Even when listening to the ritual service, or when burning incense, I always take it as a matter of course, and not surprising at all, that this flesh of mine should survive the spirit of the departed.

Someone once said to me that while the death of others seems to us but the natural thing, we cannot conceive of our own death at all. I once asked a man who had been through the war, "Can you believe that you alone will escape death, while others of your company, one after another, are falling?" His reply was, "Yes, I can. Most of them do not expect to die until they actually do." Again, I remember a conversation I had, on hearing aeroplane stories from a certain man connected with the Science Department of the University. "Since they are always thus falling and being killed, those who fly afterwards are frightened, aren't they? I suppose that they think it will be their turn next, don't they?"

"No. They don't seem to."

"Why not?"

"Why not? They seem to be governed by just the opposite psychological frame of mind. They seem to feel that, to be sure, the other fellow has fallen and been killed, but they themselves are all right."

Perhaps I, too, with the same feelings as this man, can take it with comparative calmness. It ought to be so, for everyone lives until he dies.

Strange to say, black-bordered announcements seldom come while I am sick in bed. Last fall, after recovering from my illness, I attended three or four funerals. Among these was that of Mr. Sato (of this Newspaper). I remember Mr. Sato, at a certain banquet, bringing a silver cup which he had received from the Company, and offering me wine in it. I still recall the strange dance which he performed at that time. More often than not, when attending the funeral ceremonies of such strong and healthy men, I find nothing specially strange in the fact that I should survive them. But now and then, when I come to think of it, I feel as if it were an unnatural thing that I should be alive. I have a faint suspicion that perhaps Fate is purposely playing a trick on me.

XXIII

In the neighborhood of my present residence there is a street called Kikui Cho. As this was my birthplace, I know it better than most folks. But having left home, by the time I returned from my many wanderings, this Kikui Cho had stretched out considerably, somehow or other reaching as far as Negoro.

The name of this street, so closely related to me, perhaps because I was too accustomed to hearing it in my childhood, comes to me with no sweet sound, such as would call up my past. But, sitting alone in my study, resting my cheek upon my hand, I give my mind free play, like a boat floating down the stream; and my thoughts, resting upon the four characters *Ki, Ku, I, Cho,* begin to play about them for a time.

This street seems probably not to have been in existence in the old Yedo days. Whether it was at the time Yedo was changed to Tokyo or much later than that, I do not know the exact date, but at any rate my father certainly originated the name. As our family crest was a chrysanthemum within a well-frame, he used that idea, adding "chrysanthemum" (*kiku*) to "well" (*i*), and so called it Kikui Cho. This story, whether I heard it from the lips of my father, or was told it by someone else, still remains in my memory. My father, after the office of Headman was changed to that of Ward Chief, held that position for a time, and perhaps had the privilege of naming the street. But thinking now of the proud-spirited way in which he boasted of it, all disagreeable feeling has long since vanished, and I simply indulge in a smile.

My father, moreover, gave his own family name, Natsume, to the long slope which one must ascend on going south from his house. Unfortunately this did not become as famous as the name Kikui Cho, and only the name Slope survives. But someone recently came and told me that on looking up the names of places hereabouts on the map, he found the name Natsume-zaka. So that it may be that the name which my father gave it is still in some use.

When I came back to Waseda, it was I don't know how many years after leaving Tokyo. It was before I had moved to my present residence, and I am not certain whether it was while I was out house-hunting, or on my way back from an excursion, but I accidentally, after all these years, came out at the side of my old home. As I then could see, from the street, a few of the old tiles on the second story roof, I simply thought that the old home must still be standing, and passed on, leaving things just as they were.

After I had moved to Waseda, I went once more to pass the gate. As I looked in at the front, all seemed to be unchanged, but on the gate post, to my surprise, was hanging the sign of a boarding house. I wanted to see the old Waseda rice fields, but they had already become a town. I wanted one glimpse of the tea fields and bamboo groves of Negoro, but I could not find a trace of them anywhere. I tried to guess at their whereabouts, but whether my guess was right or wrong, I could not even tell.

I stood there blankly. Why should my house stand there alone, like a relic of the past ? Within my heart I felt that it were better for it to quickly crumble away.

Time is Power. Last year, when I was taking a walk in the direction of Takada, I happened to pass that way; and noticed that our house had been demolished, and in its place a new boarding house was under construction. Beside it was a pawn shop. In front of the pawn shop was a rude enclosure, in which some trees were planted. The three pine trees had their branches closely trimmed, so that they almost seemed dwarfed. But they stirred in me a feeling of having seen them somewhere before. As I went back home I wondered whether an old poem, "O moonlight Night, casting the irregular shadows of the three pines !" might not have referred to these pine trees.

XXIV

"Having been born in such a place, have you been able to get along safely hitherto?"

"O, in one way and another I have managed to get through safely."

This word "safely" which we were using, did not mean the having of love affairs, but referred to the very opposite condition. However, my inquisitive mind could not rest satisfied with such a simple answer as this.

"It is often said that one who works at a candy store, however fond he may be of candy, soon finds it distasteful. You can understand this even from the making of rice balls at home in the equinoctial festival time, can't you? Those who prepare them, just from packing the balls in the boxes, look as if they were already satiated. Is your condition like that ?"

"No. It doesn't seem that way. At any rate until I was past twenty I was without any anxiety over it."

This man was, in one sense, a handsome man.

"Even though you, on your part, were undisturbed, it does not necessarily follow that the other party also was indifferent. In such case it would be but natural that you should be influenced as well."

"When I look back upon it now, I cannot escape many thoughts of how many things, sure enough, might be construed as having had certain meanings."

"Then you were altogether unmindful of these things, weren't you?"

"I suppose so. But there was one thing I was mindful of. Yet my heart could by no means find attraction in this other person."

I wondered if that were the end of his story. The New Year tea tables were placed before us both. But my guest did not drink at all, and I hardly took my cup in my hand, so there was absolutely no exchange of drinks.

"Is this just the way things have gone on till now?" I asked him, to make certain, while sipping my soup. My guest then suddenly rehearsed this story to me.

"At the time when I was still in employ, I was meeting a certain girl for about two years. She of course was not of the laity. But she is no longer living. She took her own life by hanging. She was nineteen. At the time she died I had not met her for about ten days. This girl, you see, was the mistress of two men, both of whom, out of jealousy, entered into competition to buy her off. Moreover, both of them seem to have made friends with her matron, and to have made it very hard for her, each urging her to come to him and not to the other ...."

"And you could not rescue her?"

"I was then but little more than a shop boy, and could do absolutely nothing."

"But did not this geisha die because of you?"

"Well ... Perhaps it was because she could not perform

— 73 —

her duty to both of these men at the same time .... And yet it is true that there was an agreement between the two of us that she should not go anywhere else."

"Then, perhaps, indirectly, you killed that girl."

"Maybe so."

"Don't you waken in the morning with troubled thoughts?"

"Yes, they aren't very happy."

My parlor, so crowded on New Year's day, was lonely and still on this the day after. I sat among the lonely pine decorations of the New Year, listening to this sad tale from my New Year's caller. And serious-minded and honest man that he was, he used almost no amorous words at all in the telling.

XXV

This is a story of the time when I was still in Sendagi, so that from the chronological standpoint it must be now quite ancient.

One day, as I was returning from a walk in the direction of Kiritoshi, instead of coming out at the corner of Hongo 4 Chome, I turned north into the first little street this side. In those days, at that corner, just next to the restaurant, a story-teller's sign was always hanging.

As this was a rainy day, I was, of course, holding an umbrella. It was a wide-spreading umbrella of a steel-blue hue, and the drops leaking down from above, naturally ran down the wooden rod and began to soak my hand. This deserted narrow street had all its mud washed away by the rain, and almost no dirt clung to the cleats of my clogs. But, even so, when I looked above, all was dark; when I looked below, all was lonesome. Perhaps it was because I was accustomed to pass there that not a solitary thing attracted my notice. And my own heart closely resembled the weather and my surroundings. I had a constant unhappy feeling, as though it would corrode my very heart. With melancholy mien I walked blankly on, in the midst of the falling rain.

When I reached the front of the story-teller's at Hikage Cho, I suddenly had to pass a covered rikisha. As nothing intervened between me and the rikisha I could tell from a distance that the person riding in it was a woman. As it was a time when the celluloid windows were not yet in vogue, the white face of the occupant of the rikisha was exposed to view from afar.

To my eyes the white face was very beautiful. While walking along in the rain, I was carried away by her appearance. At the same time the idea that she must be a geisha possessed my mind almost as if I knew it to be a fact. Then when the rikisha came to within six feet of me, the beautiful person at whom I was looking, suddenly offered me a courteous greeting. Then she passed on. On seeing her greeting, together with her smile, I for the first time realized that it was Ōtsuka Kusuo San.

The next time I met her it was some days later, and when she said to me, "Excuse me for not stopping the other day," I felt like telling her exactly how things were.

"I was really looking at you and wondering what beautiful lady it might be. I thought that perhaps you were a geisha."

What Kusuo San then replied I have no clear memory, but she did not blush at all, nor did she show any ill feeling. I thought that she took my words at their face value.

Long after that Kusuo San one day came to Waseda purposely to call. However, my wife and I had been having an unfortunate quarrel, and I sat stiffly in my study, with an ugly look. Kusuo San left after about ten minutes' conversation with my wife.

Things went thus that day, but soon thereafter I went to Nishikata Machi to apologize.

"To tell the truth we had been quarrelling. I am afraid that my wife, too, was impolite. I felt that it would have been discourteous to have shown such a cross face, so purposely withdrew myself."

Kusuo San's answer to this is now a matter of so long ago, and it has sunk so deep in the recesses of my memory that I can hardly call it forth again.

It was, I think, while I was in a hospital for stomach diseases that the news of Kusuo San's death reached me. I can remember that I was asked by telephone whether they might not use my name in the death notice. In the hospital I composed a memorial verse, "Toss in the chrysanthemums, all there are, into the casket." Some one, fond of short poems, was so pleased with this that he came to ask me to write it on a paper slip which he took away with him. That, too, was long, long ago.

XXVI

I do not know how it was that Masu San became so poverty-stricken. At any rate the Masu San whom I knew was a postman. His younger brother, Sho San, went through his property, dropped down into my home, and lived off me; but he was of higher social position than Masu San. He was always telling about how, when he was a boy, working at a fishmonger's in Honcho, he had won the favor of a Yokohama foreigner, who offered to take him abroad with him, but he had declined. Thinking of it now, he regretted not having accepted.

They were cousins on my mother's side. And because of this connection, Masu San, in order to meet his brother, as well as to show respect to my father, came about once a month to call at our home in the rear section of Ushi-gome, bringing in his hand some such small gift as a bag of *sembei* (crackers).

Masu San, at that time, had a home somewhere on the edge of Shiba or near Shinagawa, and as he seemed to live a solitary and care-free existence, he often staid all night when he came to see us. Sometimes as he was about to leave, my elder brothers would gather about him and threaten him with some such words as, "If you leave now, you will be sorry for it."

In those days my second and third brothers were still attending the Nanko school. This school was situated on the present site of the Higher Commercial School, and seems to have been established so that its graduates might enter the Kaisei School, which is the present University. When evening came they would place their hardwood desks in the hall-way and prepare their next day's lessons. Though I use the word "prepare," it was far different from the custom of the students of today. They would read a paragraph from some such book as Goodrich's English History, and then, laying the book down on the desk, would try to repeat what they had just read.

When their studies were over, Masu San would gradually become a sine qua non with them. Sho San, too, would mysteriously appear. My eldest brother, too, when he was in good humor, would take the trouble to come to the hall-way from his rear apartment. Then, when they all got together, they would begin to have fun with Masu San.

Masu San, you sometimes deliver letters at foreigners', don't you?"

"That's my business, so I have to, whether I like it or not. Yes, I do."

"Masu San, do you understand English?"

"If I could understand English I wouldn't be doing this sort of thing, would I?"

"But you have to shout out 'Mail' or something like that, don't you?"

"Yes, but Japanese is alright for that. Nowadays even foreigners can understand Japanese."

"Yes, but they say something, don't they?"

"Of course they do. Someone like Mrs. Perry can greet me in good Japanese: 'Thank you, you are alright'."

They all lead Masu San up to this point, and then burst into laughter. And then, asking him over and over again, "Masu San, what is it that the lady says?" they contrive everlastingly to make him a laughing stock. Masu San, finally, with a grim smile, would stop repeating, "You are alright". Then someone would begin to beg, "Then, Masu San, try 'The Lone Pine in the Field'."

"You say, Try, but that is more easily said than done."

"Anyhow, go on. 'Finally when he came to where the lone pine stood in the wood,' isn't it?"

But even so, Masu San, in smiles, declined to take it up. So I really never heard Masu San's Lone Pine in the Field. As I think of it now, I wonder if it were not a line from a knight's tale or a love story.

About the time I reached manhood Masu San stopped coming to the house. It seems likely that he died. If he were living, we should have had some word from him. But if his death was a fact, I have no idea when it occurred.

XXVII

I have but little acquaintance with the theatre. I am particularly ignorant of the old drama. I sometimes think that it is because I do not understand the theatrical conventions that have developed along these lines from the past, and so lack the ability to merge myself into the special world spread upon the stage. Not only that. But when I see the old drama, what seems to me most strange is to have the actors walking about between the natural and the unnatural, without belonging to either. Perhaps that is the real reason why it stirs up in me an unsettled feeling, something like a half-sitting posture.

But when a child comes out on the stage, and tells a story in a high-pitched voice, even I, all unconsciously, find my eyes filling with tears. But immediately I have a repentant thought, as having been deceived, and I wonder why I should have shed such cheap tears.

"Think of it as I will, I hate to be cheated out of tears," I once said to a man. He, a lover of the drama, corrected me with the reply, "That is but the natural thing, isn't it? Is not the restraining of tears, on the contrary, the unnatural thing?"

As I could not agree with this opinion, I tried in various ways to explain it to him. Meanwhile our conversation somehow turned to the subject of art. I had heard that he was greatly delighted with the work of Jakuchu which was recently exhibited in the Art Society, and intended to publish a criticism of it in some magazine. But again I did not much like his picture of chickens, and so, here too, as in the case of the theatre, there arose a discussion between us.

At last I flung at him the words, "After all, you have no qualification for criticizing a picture." Then, taking this statement as a basis, he began to argue that all arts have a single principle. To state briefly his main points; since all arts spring from the same source, if only we master one of them, the others naturally become easy of comprehension. Among those who sat about us not a few endorsed his statement.

"Then one who writes a novel would naturally be good at jiu-jitsu," I said, half in jest.

He laughingly replied, "But jiu-jitsu is not a fine art."

Arts do not proceed from a common source. Even if they did, it is only when they reach differentiation that the flowers can bloom. And so, if we restore them to their primitive state, pictures, sculpture, literature, all come to absolute nothing. There can be no common element there. Even if there were, it could be of no practical use. It would be impossible to find any concrete thing in common among them.

This was my line of argument at that time. And it was by no means a satisfactory one. There was abundant room for me to have accepted his assertion, and to have given him a thoughtful explanation.

But one of those who sat near suddenly took up my argument, and began to attack the other with it. So I was too weary to pursue it further. But this fellow who took up my cudgels was quite drunk. He kept arguing about art and literature and so forth, but he did not say anything that got anywhere. His very use of words was inarticulate. Those who at first were interested and amused, gradually became silent.

The intoxicated fellow ended by saying, " Our friendship ends here."

To this I replied, "Well, end your friendship out-doors. This is no place for it."

"Then let us go out and finish it outside," the drunken man said in consultation with the other. But the opponent made no move to go, so things went no further.

This occurred on the first day of the year. The man who was intoxicated often comes to see me, but he never mentions the quarrel of that day.

XXVIII

Someone, on seeing our cat, asked me what generation it belonged to, and I answered, without giving it thought, "It is of the second generation." But on further consideration I realized that the second generation had already passed, and this was of the third.

Its ancestor of the first generation, in spite of being homeless, had in one sense become rather famous, but on the contrary, the life of the second in line was so brief as to have been forgotten, even by its master. I do not know very well who brought it, or from where it came, but I still recall the time when it would creep about, its form tiny enongh to rest in the palm of my hand. This cunning creature lost its life by having some one of the household trample upon it one morning when the beds were being put away. Hearing a plaintive cry they promptly drew it out from its hiding place under the quilt, and gave it proper treatment, but it was too late. A day or two afterwards, it died. And its successor is the jet black one of the present time.

As for this black cat, I neither like it nor dislike it. The cat, too, on its part, just prowls about the house, and has never shown any inclination to come to me.

One day it crept into the kitchen cupboard and fell into a pot. As that pot happened to be full of sesame oil, its body began to glisten as if it had been smeared with cosmetics. With that shining body it lay down on my manuscript, and the oil soaked through it, clear to the bottom, much to my annoyance.

Last year, just before I fell sick, it suddenly contracted a skin disease. From its face and forehead the hair gradually fell off. And as it was always scratching with its claws, the scabs kept falling, leaving bare red patches. One day, while having my meal, I was gazing with a disagreeable look at this disgusting condition.

I said to the members of the household, "O, it is shedding scabs. It would be too bad for the children to catch the infection. Better take it to the hospital and give it prompt treatment." But I inwardly thought that, especially since the disease was of such a nature, it might not recover. I recalled that a long time ago a foreigner of my acquaintance was very fond of a fine dog which he had received from a certain count, and somehow it had been attacked by this same skin disease, and so he, out of pity for it, had called a doctor and had it killed.

"It would be less painful and more fortunate for the cat if we should kill it with some such thing as chloroform."

I repeated these words three or four times, but before the cat had carried out my wishes in the matter, I myself had to go to bed, sick. During that period I had no opportunity at all to see it. Perhaps because my own suffering took direct control over me, I had no margin of strength for thinking of the sickness of the other.

Not until October was I barely able to leave the bed. Then, as usual, I saw the black form. But, strangely enough, upon its ugly red bare skin, the black fur had begun to grow as of old. "Well, I wonder if it will recover."

During my weary convalescence I continually let my eyes rest upon it. And as I gradually recuperated, its hair, too, became thick. And after it became normal again, it began to grow fatter than ever.

When I compared the course of my own illness with that of the cat, I sometimes had a hint that there might be some connection between the two. But then I immediately realize how foolish it is, and only smile. As for the cat, it only meows, so I could have no idea what its feelings were.

XXIX

I am a so-called last child, born in my parents' later years. Even now the story is often repeated of how, when I was born, mother said that she was ashamed to have a child at such an age. It may not have been alone for that reason, but immediately after my birth my parents sent me away to be brought up. Of course I would hardly be expected to remember this foster home, but when, in my manhood, I made inquiries about it, I learned that it was with a poor couple, who made a living by dealing in second-hand furniture.

Tucked in a little basket, alongside this man's odds and ends of furniture, I was nightly exposed in the way-side shop on the main street of Yotsuya. One night, my elder sister, happening to pass by, caught sight of me, and, perhaps out of pity, putting me in her bosom, took me home with her. But I could not sleep that night, and kept crying all night long, so that my sister was roundly scolded by my father.

I do not know when it was that I was taken back from this foster home. But I was immediately sent away again, to be adopted into a certain family. I am pretty sure it was when I was four. I grew up there until I reached eight or nine, the age of discretion, and then, as some strange trouble arose in my adopted home, it resulted in my again returning to my own home.

Transferred from Asakusa to Ushigome, I was all unconscious that I was returning to my real home, and still thought that my parents were my grandparents, and did not think it at all strange to call them grandfather and grandmother, as usual. They, too, perhaps thinking it wrong to correct my former habits abruptly, kept their faces unconcerned, while I was calling them thus.

Unlike the common case of youngest children, I was not at all beloved by my parents. This arose from several causes, perhaps from my being of a disobedient nature, or from having been separated from my parents for such a long time. The memory stays with me of having been rather cruelly treated by my father. In spite of this, for some unknown reason, I was overjoyed at being removed from Asakusa to Ushigome. And my joy was so openly expressed that everyone could see it.

In my folly I thought that my real parents were my grandparents, and how long I persisted in this belief I cannot tell. But one night, this is what happened.

While in my bed in a room, alone, someone at my pillow kept calling my name in a soft voice. I awoke in surprise, but all about was in total darkness. I could not quite tell who it was that was crouching there, but being a child I simply listened to what the other had to say. Then, while I was listening, I realized that it was the voice of our maid servant. She, in the darkness, as if whispering to my ear, spoke as follows:

"Those whom you think to be your grandfather and grandmother are in fact your father and mother. A little while ago I heard them talking, and saying that that was probably why you like this house, and how strange it is, and such like. So I have come quietly to tell you. You mustn't let any one know. Promise ? "

"I won't tell anybody," was all I then said, but in my heart there was a great joy. That joy was mine, not because of the thing that she had told me, but simply because of her kindness.

XXX

As I sit thus in my study most of my callers ask me, "Have you completely recovered from your illness?" Though asked the same question so many times, just so often I hesitate to answer. And in the end I always come to repeat the same words, no other than this strange response, "Well, in one way or another I manage to keep alive."

I manage to keep alive — I have used this one sentence for a long time, but as often as I use it, I somehow have an uncanny feeling, and wonder if I should not really give it up; and yet I cannot find elsewhere any suitable words for expressing the condition of my health.

One day, when Mr. T. called, I told him about this, and said that I didn't know what other answer to give, since I couldn't tell whether I should recover or not. Mr. T. then promptly offered this reply.

"Then you can't say that you've recovered, can you? There seem to be such frequent relapses. You might call this a continuation of your original illness."

On hearing the word "continuation" I felt as if I had heard just the right word. So thereafter I gave up replying, "Well, in one way or another I manage to keep alive," and revised it to, "My sickness is still in continuation." And whenever I explained the meaning of "continuation," I always used the Great European War as an illustration.

"Just as Germany is fighting against the Allied armies, I am making war against my sickness. That you and I can sit here face to face is not because peace has come, but because I have climbed down into a trench and am keeping my gaze fixed upon my enemy, illness. My body is a world in conflict. There is no telling when a change may come, or of what nature it will be."

Some, on hearing my explanation, laugh heartily, as if it were entertaining; others remain silent; still others look sorry for me.

After my callers had gone, I reflected further. "Things in continuation" are not necessarily limited to my illness. I wonder whether there may not be, to some extent, hidden away in the back of the minds of those who hear my explanation — those who laugh, thinking it a joke; those who are silent, as not understanding; those who look sorry, from sympathetic thoughts — all unknown to me and not realized by themselves, some things that are "in continuation". If these should explode all at once, with a great report, resounding in their breast, what would they think? Their memory at that time would have nothing to tell them. Their consciousness of the past would already have gone.

Since they cannot recognize any relation between the present, the past, and the remote past, how will they interpret them when they come to such a pass ? After all, do we not all walk smilingly to that far place called Death, each of us holding a bomb made in our own dreams? Is it not fortunate that neither we nor anyone else can know what it is that we are holding?

When I realized that my sickness might be in continuation, I also wondered whether the European War might not be a continuation from some past age. However, the question of whence and how it began, or how it will eventuate, is altogether beyond me; and I rather envy those people who cannot understand the word "continuation".

XXXI

When I was still young, going to Primary School, I had a chum called Kii-Chan. Kii-Chan, in those days, was living in his uncle's home in Naka-Cho, and as it was some little distance from my home, I could not go to see him every day. As a rule I did not go out to him, but waited at home for him to visit me. Regardess of my failure to visit him, he was always sure to come. The place of our rendezvous was a stationery shop which Matsu San rented from us.

Kii-Chan seemed to have no parents, but to my childish mind there seemed to be nothing strange about that. It may be that I never inquired, and so never knew the reason why he came to Matsu San's house. It was long afterwards that I learned this story. I heard that his father, when he was an officer of some kind or other, in Ginza, in olden days, came under the suspicion of counterfeiting, and was sent to prison where he died. Later on, his surviving widow left Kii-Chan in the home of her former husband and married Matsu San, and so it was but natural that Kii-Chan should sometimes go to visit his own mother.

In my childish ignorance, these circumstances, even if I heard them, made hardly any impression upon me, and so, when frolicking about with Kii-Chan, I never gave a thought to his circumstances.

We both were fond of Chinese classics, and in spite of not understanding them, found much pleasure in arguing over them. He often amazed me by giving the names of difficult classics, names he had learned by hearing, or by looking them up.

One day he came into our entry, which was at the same time my room, and drew from his bosom a two volume set of books, which he showed me. I remember that they were in manuscript form, and in the Chinese style of composition. I took the volumes from him and turned the pages over aimlessly here and there. To tell the truth, I hadn't the slightest idea of what they were about. But Kii-Chan was too courteous to ask me whether or not I understood them.

"This is the handwriting of Nampo Ota. My friend says that he wants to sell them, so I came to show them to you. Won't you buy them?"

I didn't know who Nampo Ota might be.

"Who is Nampo Ota, anyway?"

"Why, Shoku-San-Jin. That famous Shoku-San-Jin."

In my ignorance, I did not even know the name of Shoku-San-Jin. But when I was told this by Kii-Chan, I felt that these must be valuable books.

"How much would you sell them for?" I ventured to ask.

"He said that he would sell them for fifty sen. How about it?"

I stopped to consider. However, it struck me as the best policy to bargain him down a bit.

"I'd take them for twenty five sen."

"Alright. Twenty five sen will satisfy him. So please take them."

While saying this Kii-Chan took the twenty five sen from me, and kept on praising the merits of the books. As, of course, I couldn't understand them, I wasn't specially elated over the matter, but at least had the satisfaction of probably not having lost anything. That night I placed on my desk the Shugen Nampo; (that was the name, if I remember correctly) and went to sleep.

XXXII

The next day Kii-Chan came ambling in.

"It's about the books you bought from me yesterday."

That was all Kii-Chan said, and remained hesitant looking at my face. I let my eyes rest on the books lying on my desk.

"Those books? Well, what about those books? "

"What I had done became known to the old man of that house, and he became much enraged, and wanted me to come to you and get them back. I hated to do it, after having turned them over to you, but there was no help for it, so here I am again."

"To take back the books? "

"Well, I wouldn't just say, 'take them'; but if you don't mind, would you please return them to me? Anyway, they say that twenty five sen is too cheap."

At these last words a distinct feeling of uneasiness, which had been vaguely hidden away behind my satisfaction at having bought them cheap, began to dawn upon me — an uneasiness arising from my having done a wrong act. So besides being angry with my lower self, I was, on the other hand, angry at him for having sold them to me for twenty five sen. How could I pacify both these angry feelings at the same time? I sat silent for a time with a bitter face.

As for this psychological state, since I now recall myself then as a child and analyze it, I can depict it with comparative clearness, but to me at that time it was altogether beyond understanding. The only result that I was conscious of was my having a bitter face. Of course Kii-Chan would not be expected to know more than that. Perhaps I should say this in parenthesis, but even today, in my maturity, such things often happen to me, and I am often misunderstood by others.

Kii-Chan looked up at my face and said, "Twenty five sen is really too cheap."

I promptly took the books that were lying on the desk and threw them before Kii-Chan.

"Then, I'll give them back."

"I'm sorry, but I can't help it. They don't belong to Yasu-ko anyway. He says that in order to get pin money he was secretly selling what had been in his father's home from olden times."

I was so wrathy that I made no reply. Kii-Chan took twenty five sen from his sleeve, and was about to put it before me, but I made no move to touch it.

"I won't take such money."

"Why?"

"Never mind why, but I won't."

"Is that so? But aren't you unreasonable just to return the books? Since you return the books won't you take the twenty five sen? "

It was more than I could stand.

"The books are mine. If I have once bought them, doesn't that make them mine?"

"That's true enough. True enough, but the other folks are troubled."

"That's why I am returning them, isn't it? But that's no reason why I should take the money."

"Don't talk such nonsense. Please take it."

"I'll give them to you. They are my books, but if you want them, I say you can have them. Since I give them to you, isn't it enough just to have them?"

"Well, alright. Let it be that way, then."

Kii-Chan finally went home with just the books. And for no reason whatever I was deprived of my twenty five sen pin money.

XXXIII

As a member of the human race in this world I cannot possibly pursue a solitary existence. There naturally arises somewhere the necessity for associating with others. Greetings of the season, business conferences, and even more complicated dealings — it is difficult for me to avoid these things, however simple a life I live.

I wonder whether I should accept everything that people tell me as true, accepting all their words and deeds at their face value. If I should take no further thought than to entrust myself to this naturally simple disposition of mine, I might sometimes be deceived by those whom I do not suspect. As a result I might be made fun of and sneered at behind my back. And it is not impossible that, in extreme cases, I might receive unendurable insults before my very face.

If, on the other hand, I regard all men as unconscionable liars, and from the very start refuse to listen to their words or to incline my heart to them, sometimes finding the opposite meaning hidden away beneath the surface, could I deem myself a wise man and find there a place where I could live on in peace? In that case I might misjudge others. Moreover, from the beginning I must go on the conscious assumption that I may commit fatal errors. Sometimes, as a natural result it would go hard if I did not make a bold face, sufficient even to insult an innocent person.

If I try to adjust my attitude to one or the other of these aspects, a certain difficulty arises in my mind. I do not want to trust unworthy men. Nor do I want to injure good men. And of those who appear before me, I cannot think that all are unworthy, nor again that all are good. And so my attitude must vary in accordance with those who come.

I suppose this change of attitude is necessary for all, and is also being put in practice by every one, but I wonder if, after all, it aptly fits the other person, or whether it can walk fearlessly upon the delicate line, without deviating the fraction of an inch. My great question always lurks thereabouts.

Not counting my prejudice, I have bitter memories of past experiences of having been fooled by many people. At the same time I wonder if there have not been frequent occasions when, not taking the words and deeds of the other at face value, I have interpreted them in no other way than would put shame upon his character.

My attitude toward others comes first from the experiences I have hitherto had; then from the attending circumstances and the surrounding conditions; and last of all, though the words may be ambiguous, the instinct given me from above has some part in it. So that sometimes I am fooled by the other, sometimes I fool him, and in rare cases I give him just the proper treatment.

But my previous experience, though it seems broad, is exceedingly narrow. It often happens that an experience which I have repeated over and over in one stratum of society, taken to another stratum is altogether useless. In the matter of the attendant circumstances and surrounding conditions, since they are so varied, it is not only that the bounds of their application are limited, but also they are useless unless one gives them varied consideration. However, in most cases there is not sufficient time or material for such consideration.

So sometimes I like to judge others chiefly on the basis of my own very dubious intuition, whose reality I am never certain of. And it often happens that I have no opportunity to prove whether my intuition was, after all, right or wrong, by what is, in short, an objective fact. Here, also my doubts are always overhanging, like a mist, oppressing my heart.

If there is an all-wise and almighty God in the world, I kneel before this God and pray that He will give me intuition so clear that there will be no room for the slightest doubt, and will save me from this agony. If not I pray that He will grant me the happiness of fitting my soul to those of others, changing into men of transparent honesty all those who appear before my ignorant self. At present I feel as if there were only three alternatives — that I be made a fool of by others, that in the depth of my mistrust I cannot really take others in, or that I am filled with anxiety, gloom, and unhappiness. If this should continue life long, how unfortunate we mortals would be!

XXXIV

A certain university graduate, whom I had taught while there, came to me and said, "I hear you delivered a lecture at the Higher Technical School." I replied, "Yes, I did." He then said to me, "They say they couldn't understand you at all."

Up to that time, in regard to my speaking, I had never had any apprehension along that line at all, but on hearing these words of his I was struck with misgivings.

"How did you know that?"

His answer to this question was quite simple. Whether relative or merely acquaintance I am not sure, but a young man in a certain home with which he was connected, was a student at that school and heard my lecture that day, and this young man had reported the matter to him in the words, "I couldn't understand anything."

"Well, what did you lecture about?"

I repeated to him, right there, the main points of my lecture.

"You don't think that is specially difficult, do you? Why couldn't he understand it?"

"They probably couldn't understand it. No, they surely couldn't get that."

This positive answer sounded exceedingly strange to me. But what made me feel all the worse was the regretful thought that it had been better if I had not lectured at all.

To tell the truth, time and again I had been invited by this school to give a lecture, and time and again had declined. So that when finally I gave consent, it was with a hope in my heart that I might give something worth while to the audience that should be gathered there. When I saw this hope absolutely crushed by his simple words, "No, they surely couldn't get that," I couldn't help thinking that my taking all the trouble to go to Asakusa had been useless.

This is now an old story, of a year or two back; but last fall, having tried in vain to escape giving a lecture at a certain school, I at length went to do so, and suddenly recalled my regrets of the previous year. Moreover, the subject which I was then to discuss contained material not easy for the young audience to comprehend, and so, just before I left the platform, I said,

"I think there is probably no misunderstanding, but if there is anything in what I have just said which is not clear, please come and call on me. I will explain to your satisfaction, in so far as I am able."

I had almost no notion at that time as to what effect this would have upon them. But it is a fact that three or four days later three young men visited me in my study. Of these, two had made appointment with me by telephone. The third wrote a courteous letter, asking me to fix a time to meet him.

I cordially received these young men, and inquired the purpose of their coming. One of them, as I had expected, had questions along the line of my lecture; but the other two, to my surprise, had come to ask about the attitude a friend of theirs should take regarding his family. So they had brought their immediate, pressing problem of how best to apply my lecture to practical life.

For the benefit of these three I said what I thought should be said, and explained what I thought needed explanation. Of course, judging from the result, I could not tell how much profit this gave them, but at least I was far more satisfied than when I was told that people said they couldn't understand my lecture.

(Two or three days later, when this article appeared in the paper, I received four or five letters from students of the Higher Technical School. All of them had heard my lecture, and had written in refutation of the statement, so as to dispel the disappointment I had here recorded. And so these letters were all filled with goodwill. And not one wrote in criticism of my having hastily judged the opinion of the whole audience by the words of one student. So I add this word here, in apology for my own density, and at the same time publicly expressing my thanks to those who rectified my mistake.)

XXXV

When I was a boy, I often used to go to hear the stories at a professional story-teller's called Isemoto, in Setomono Cho, Nihonbashi. Just opposite the present Mitsukoshi Store there was always hanging a sign announcing the day performance, and, turning that corner, a short half cho on the right hand side brought one to the storyteller's. As the evening performances dealt with romantic affairs only, I never set foot there except in daytime; but as to the frequency of my visits, I think I went there more often than anywhere else. Of course my home at that time was not the one below Takata-no-Baba. However easily accessible it may have been, it seems strange to me, when I think of it, that I had so much time to spend in going to hear the story-telling.

It may be because I look back upon it as remote past, but this place, for a story-teller's, seemed to have for its patrons an air of respectability. On the right hand side of the platform a section was set off by low lattice partitions, and within it seats were provided for the regular patrons. Behind the platform was a porch way, and behind that a garden. Within the garden an old plum tree projected out on a slant above the well curb, and occupied just space enough so that when one looked out from the porch way, the sky could be seen with no feeling of restriction. In the eastern part of the garden also could be seen a building, like a detached villa.

As those in the latticed section were wealthy folks and had spare time on their hands, they were all properly dressed, and would frequently, with ennui, take their hair pincers from their sleeves, and patiently pull out hairs from their noses. On such a tranquil day I enjoyed a feeling as if a nightingale were come and singing in the plum tree in the garden.

It was the custom at this house for the boy who sells tea and boxed cakes, during the intermission, to go about distributing these among the patrons. The boxes were shallow and oblong, and were placed here and there, within reach of any who might wish them. As for the number of the cakes, I think there were ten to a box. And there was a tacit understanding that any who wished might eat them, and leave the money in the box. At that time I looked upon such an unusual custom as this as an interesting thing, but now, when I look about and think that one cannot find in any story-teller's today, such an open-hearted and care-free spirit, it all seems very dear to me.

In such an old quiet atmosphere I heard various people tell the ancient tales. Among these was one man who used such strange expressions as Sutotoko, nonnon, zuizui. He was called Nanryu Tanabe, and the story was that he had once checked clogs somewhere. These words, Sutotoko, nonnon, zuizui, were famous, but no one knew what they meant. He seemed to have used them as adjectives in describing the advance of armies.

This Nanryu has been dead many years. Most of the others, too, have passed away. And knowing nothing at all about later circumstances, I have absolutely no idea how many of those who then entertained me may now be living.

Once when I attended a year-end meeting of the Bi-On-Kwai (Harmony Club), on examining the program, I found, among all the numbers arranged there, such as the farce by the Yoshiwara clowns, only one friend from those old days. I went to the Shin-Tomi-Za, and saw him there. I also heard his voice, and was surprised to find that there was not the slightest change in looks or voice from olden times. His story, too, was exactly as of old. Though he had made no progress, neither had he gone backward. Deeply conscious of the radical changes in this twentieth century, in both myself and my surroundings, I sat before him, lost in a kind of meditation, ever in my heart contrasting him with myself.

This man was known as Bakin, the same young man that had been called Kinryō in the days when he appeared in Nanryu's intermission, in the olden days at Isemoto.

XXXVI

When my eldest brother was attending the Kaiseiko, before it had become the University, he had to leave school because of lung trouble. As there was a great difference in our ages, it remains deeply impressed on my memory that our relations were more those of man and child than the ordinary intimacy of brothers. It was more especially when he was angry that this feeling seems to have been impressed upon me.

My brother was a handsome fellow, with light complexion and a high nose. But whether from his face or from his expression, he had somewhere a stern look, which gave people the feeling that they might not approach him without cause.

At the time my brother was in school it was still the period when young men were sent as students by the provincial governments, and there seems to have been here and there within the school such an atmosphere as young men of today could hardly imagine. He told me that he had once been sent a love letter by an upper class student. This upper class man seems to have been much older than my brother. I wonder what my brother did with that letter, brought up, as he was, in Tokyo where such a custom was unknown. My brother told me that thereafter, whenever he met that man in the school bath, he was overcome with embarrassment.

At the time he left school he was extremely conscientious and always assumed a strict demeanor, so that the attitude of even his father and mother was that of deference. In addition, perhaps on account of his sickness, he always kept himself shut in, with gloomy looks.

I don't know when it was, but he began to soften and his disposition naturally grew gentle, and he got to going out at night-fall, clad in an old taffeta kimono and stiff girdle. He would sometimes leave in the tea room pretty fans from the Kamesei Restaurant decorated on one side with purple hexagon forms. This in itself was not so bad, but he would sit before the long brazier incessantly imitating the voice of the professional. However, those in the house did not seem to pay any special attention to it. I, of course, was unconcerned. Along with the feigned voice began also the tōhachi hand game. But as this required an opponent it could not be repeated every night. But anyway he would eagerly raise or lower his strangely awkward hands. My third eldest brother seems to have served most often as his opponent. All I could do was to look on, with serious face.

This eldest brother finally died of tuberculosis. If my memory does not fail me, it was in 1887 that he died. Then when the funeral was over and the night after cremation past, and when we thought everything was completed, a certain woman called. My third brother went out to receive her, and she inquired of him as follows:

"Your brother remained unmarried until death, didn't he ?"

My brother, because of his illness, had remained single all his life.

"Yes. He remained single until the end."

"I am relieved to hear that. People like myself cannot get along at all without a husband. There is no help for it, but ..."

This woman who had come all the way from Kōshū, left after learning the name of the temple where my brother's ashes had been interred. I then heard for the first time the story of how, when she had been a geisha at Yanagi-Bashi my brother had had relations with her.

I will not deny that I sometimes wish I might meet her and talk things over with her about my brother. But I suppose that if I should meet her, I would find her an old lady, with looks altogether different from of old. And perhaps her heart, too, like her face, would be withered and hardened to a crust. And if that were so, for her to meet me, his younger brother, would, I suppose, bring her only pain and sadness.

XXXVII

I should like to write here something in memory of my mother, but unfortunately but little material remains in my memory of the mother whom I knew.

Mother was called Chiye, and I still count this word, Chiye, as a very precious one. I feel as if it were the name of my mother alone, and could not be the name of any other woman. Happily, I have never met any woman of the name of Chiye, other than my mother.

Mother died when I was thirteen or fourteen years old, but the image of her which I call up from the now long ago, however I try to pursue the thread of my memory, seems to be that of an old woman. Born as I was in her later years, I was never given the privilege of remembering her youthful beauty.

The mother whom I knew used to sew with big spectacles on. Those spectacles were old folks' iron rim style, and I suppose that the lenses were more than two inches in diameter. When mother would put them on, she would draw her chin down into her collar a little, and would often gaze steadily at me; but I, not at that time knowing the nature of old people's eyes, thought this was simply her habit. Along with these glasses I recall a pair of paper doors which mother always had for a background. Among the worn old papers pasted to these, there floats clearly before my eyes a picture of the lithographs on which were written, "Birth and Death, Things of Great Moment, Mutable, Transient, etc."

When summer came, mother would always wear a plain dark blue silk gauze kimono, with a narrow black satin girdle. Strangely enough, the picture of my mother which remains in my memory always presents itself to my mind in this summer garb alone. And if I eliminate the plain dark blue silk gauze kimono and the narrow black satin girdle, all that remains is her face. The figure of my mother, once, out on the verandah playing chess with my brother, is the only memory I possess of the two of them together; but here also she was sitting in the same kimono with the same girdle.

I never remember having been taken to mother's old home, and for a long time I lived on without knowing where she had come from. I had no curiosity at all to inquire about it for myself. Here, too, the matter must seem hazy and indefinite, but I am certain that I had heard that she had been born in Ōban Machi, Yotsuya. Her father seems to have been a pawnbroker. I seem to have been told that there were many godowns there, but never until this day having passed this Ōban Machi, I have completely forgotten such details. Even granting that this were so, the memory which I have of my mother does not reveal any estate with godowns on it. The probability is that by that time they had been demolished.

I remember dimly the story that until she married my father she had served in a palace, but which daimyo's palace she was in, or how long she had served there, is a matter almost beyond my grasp — like incense that has burned out, but still gives forth a gentle fragrance — for I have no proper understanding of the nature of service in a palace.

When this story is told, I seem to recall having seen in our godown a gorgeously decorated kimono, like those of palace maids, depicted in old colour prints. On the front of the kimono which had a red back, designs of cherry or plum were dyed, and here and there it was embroidered with gold and silver thread. Perhaps this was the *kaidori*, or flowing gown of that day, but by no stretch of the imagination can I today recall how my mother would have looked when she put it on. For the mother whom I knew was always an old lady with her spectacles on. Not only that; I later saw this gown made over into a bed covering, and thrown over someone who had been taken sick in the house.

XXXVIII

It is now long since that when a certain foreign teacher
of mine at the University was leaving Japan, I wanted
to make him some farewell gift, so took out from our
godown a beautiful writing box of embossed lacquer,
with red tassels attached. At the time I took this to my
father to obtain it from him, I did not have this thought
at all, but now while I am penning this, that writing box
too, like the gown with red back made over into a quilt,
holds for me deep memories of my mother when she was
young. It was said that mother never in her whole life had
any clothes made for her by father. I wonder whether
she had not already prepared enough to get along without receiving any. I wonder whether, when she came as a
bride, she already had in her chest a plain dark blue silk
gauze kimono and a narrow black satin girdle. I wish I
could meet mother again and hear about all these things
from her own lips.

Naughty and headstrong as I was, I was not treated
indulgently by mother, as is usual with the youngest
child. But even so, there is always mingled with my
memory of mother a strong feeling of affinity which tells
me that among all those at home the one who gave me
the greatest affection was my mother. Aside from our
kindred affection, she was surely a woman of beautiful
character, and every one admitted that she surpassed

my father in sagacity. For her alone my cranky elder brother had great respect.

"Mother doesn't say anything, but there is something awesome about her."

I can still call up clearly from the dim past these words, with which my elder brother characterized mother. But this is no more than a fragment of my treacherous memory, like the laborious restoring to their original form of square written characters, which are running into script, as though melting in water. Besides these things everything else concerning my mother is to me like a dream. However carefully I gather together the scattered traces of mother that remain, I am not able to picture her complete self. And even most of those scattered remnants of old have already faded away, and I cannot securely grasp them.

I once went upstairs and took a nap all by myself. In those days, when I took a nap I was often troubled with some mental illusion. My thumb would suddenly grow big, and would not stop, however long it might continue; the ceiling at which I was gazing while lying on my back would come down and strike me on the chest; though looking at my normal surroundings with open eyes, my body alone was the prisoner of sleep, and however I might struggle, I could not move hand or foot. It often happened that even when I thought of it afterwards I could not tell whether I had been dreaming or awake. This time, too, I was having one of these illusions.

I do not know when or where I had done the wrong, but I had used up a large amount of money that did not belong to me. Why or how I spent it, that too is not clear. But being a child I had no way of making it good, so with my tender conscience I suffered great agony in my sleep. At last in a loud voice I called for my mother downstairs. The stairs leading up to the second floor were just behind the paper doors, pasted with the lithographs, on which were written, Birth and Death, Things of Great Moment, Mutable, Transient, etc., which I cannot separate from my mother's big spectacles. As soon as she heard my voice she came right upstairs. I told her, standing there gazing at me, about my agony, and begged her to do something. Mother then smilingly replied, "Don't worry. Mother will give you all the money you need." I was overjoyed and peacefully went sound asleep.

Even now I could not be sure whether this was all a dream or half true. But somehow I cannot help feeling that I really did beg my mother to save me, crying in a loud voice, and that she really appeared and gave me words of comfort. And my mother's appearance at that time, as always seen in my eyes, was that of the plain dark blue silk gauze kimono and the narrow black satin girdle.

XXXIX

Today being Sunday, and the children not having to go to school, it seems as though the maid felt relaxation and got up later than usual. Even so, when I rose from bed it was a quarter past seven. Having washed my face and breakfasted on my usual toast and milk and soft boiled egg ...... I turned my steps toward the garden where I had not been for some time. The gardener was putting something away in the shed. The sight of three little girls warming themselves around a pile of discarded charcoal bags from which the flames were vigorously rising, attracted my attention.

"If you get so near the open fire, you will get your faces all black," I said; to which the youngest replied, "That won't do." After gazing at the roof tiles damp with the melted frost and glittering in the morning sun, visible afar above the stone wall, I went back again into the house.

Waiting for my study to be put in order, when it was cleaned by my little maid relative, I placed my desk out on the verandah. There I leaned easily against the rail in the sunlight, or meditated with my chin in my hands, or sat motionless for a while, giving my soul free play.

The faint breeze came to sway the long leaves of the potted orchid. Among the trees of the garden the awkward chirp of the baby nightingale could be heard. While

I had been seated day after day within my glass doors, thinking it still winter, spring somehow began to sway my heart.

However long I sat, my meditation never took any definite form. If I took up my pen to write, I felt as though I had any amount of subject material to write about, yet when I cast about as to whether it should be this or that, I had the idle thought that whatever I might write about would be worthless. While remaining thus for a time, I came to feel that everything I had hitherto written was altogether meaningless. A compunction as to why I should have written these began to assail me. Happily my nerves were calm. Riding upon this assault and floating up to the realm of lofty meditation became exceedingly pleasant to me. Looking down from the clouds, and wanting to laugh at my foolish disposition, I was moved by a spirit of self-condemnation, and was no better than a child sleeping in its cradle.

I have hitherto written about the affairs of others and myself in jumbled fashion. In writing of the affairs of others I have sought, as far as possible, not to annoy them. When speaking of myself, on the contrary, I have been able to breathe the air of comparative freedom. But even so, in regard to myself I have not yet reached the point where I could take all the color out of it. Though I have not the ostentatious desire to impose upon others by telling lies, neither have I exposed the baser things or the faults of which I am most ashamed. Someone has said that the Confessions of St. Augustine, the Confessions of Rousseau, the Confessions of an Opium Eater however far one may go, the true facts can never be depicted by human power. All the more in the case of mine, since my writings are not confessions. My sins, if they can be called sins, have been perhaps depicted only from the very bright side. Some may feel displeasure there. But I myself, riding above this displeasure and looking out upon the race in general, am wreathed in smiles. I likewise smile when I survey my own self with the same eye, myself the writer of these worthless things, as if I were some other man.

The nightingale still sometimes sings in the garden. The spring breeze comes to sway the leaves of the orchid, as if to recall it now and then. The cat, with its badly bitten temple, sleeps snugly, lying in the sun. The children, playing in the garden until a moment ago, sending up their rubber airships, have all gone together to the movies. While the house and my heart are quiet, I throw open my glass doors, and bathed in the calm light of spring, I dreamily finish these lines. Then I intend to bend my elbow a little, and take a nap here on the verandah.

NOTES

I

Page 3

line 3. from within my glass doors ,「確 子戸の中から」。
within には surround の意あり、従つて戸
(doors) は複數を用ふ。

3–4. my eye catches,「私の眼に着く」。eye = eye sight.

5. laden,「累々と(赤い實の)結(な)つた」。

6. soaring skyward,「空に聳ゆる」。

7. my field of vision,「私の視野」「眼界」。

14–15. I simply note the passing of the days,「私 はた、
其の日其の日の経過を心にとめる丈である」。

16. My mind has ... been stirred,
「私の頭(こしろ) は時々動く」。

22. with a glow of interest,「興味に充ち た眼をもつて」。

24. to commit to writing,「書きつける。

Page 4

line 4. scan its headlines,
「新聞の見出し(即ち大きな活 字)丈に眼を注ぐ」。

8. sensational news,「辛辣な記事」。

8–9. strained nerves,「牽張した神經」。

10. the tram stop,「電車の停留場」。

14. braving the contempt of these people,
「これ等の人々の輕蔑を冒して」。

24 . the farmers are in financial straits, the farmers are
hard up for money.

Page 5

line 1. should not project himself into the newspapers,
「新聞に顔が出せない」。
such a one といつたから himself を用ふ。

2. to crowd out,「押し出す」「押し退ける」。

4. the heart to undertake,「やるだけの膽力」。

9. the editorial scissors ,「編輯者の 言ひ換へれば「編輯者の意志」「紙面の都合」。Editor に無くてならぬものは鋏と糊 (paste) 。.

II

Page 6.

line 2. the receiver,「受話器」。

6. photo, photograph の略語。

12. its special feature,「其(雑誌) の特色」。

20. to pose with a smile, to stand before a camera with a smile.

Page 7.

lines 1-2. hung up the receiver,
「受話器 を掛けた」「電話を切つた」。

14–15. What a man to say such a foolish thing !
「馬鹿な事をいふ男だ! 」。

15. "This will do,"「是で澤山だ」「是で好いだらう」。

25. artificial means,「人工的手段」「手 を入れて」。

26. callers, visitors.

Page 8

lines 5–6.. this picture with its pained, uncanny smile,
「氣味の悪い苦笑を洩らしてるる此の寫眞」。

III

Page 9.

lines 5-6. just weaned from his mother,
「乳離れのした許りの」。

12. began to whine,「クンクン泣き出した」。

15–16. a wink of sleep ,「一睡」「まんじりとも」。

20. I could not get him out of my mind,「彼の 事を忘れる事が出来なかつた」「必ず氣に掛つた」。

22. made a play thing of him,「彼を弄 物にした」。

25–26. with the request that I give the dog a name, with
the request that I should give the dog a name.

Page 10

line 10. dragged,「引き摺つた」。

20–21. by the household, by my people.

23. a common ailment among dogs,「犬によくある病 」。

Page 11

line 4. prescribed by the physician,「醫者の命じた」。

5. had been skeptical ,「疑つてるた」「首を傾けてるた」
。at this rate,「此分なら」。

7. frisked about,「飛び廻つた」。

IV

Page 12

line 7. propensity,「性癖」。

8. recklessly,「無暗、やたらに」。

11–12. wanton destruction,「勝手な狼籍」。

18. to prowl about,「のそのそと歩き廻る」。

19–20. a police box,「交番」。

20–21. any suspicious person,「うさん臭 いもの」。

23. a lion mask dancer,「角兵衛獅子」。

Page 13

line 1. stand his ground,「一歩も退かぬ」。

7. common to his kind,「彼の種族に共通な」。

11. muddy paws ,「泥足」。

12. last summer until on into the fall,
「去年の夏 から秋にかけて」。

16–17. his figure,「彼の姿」。

18. made no response to my advances,
「私の情 (なさ) けに應じなかつた」。

Page 14

line 5. In my convalescence,「病後の私」。

6. neck band,「襟」。

— 123 —

V

Page 15.

line 6. purposely restrained myself,「わざと差し控へた」。

9. lapping up,「ぴちゃぴちゃと飲む」。

19. an atmosphere of mutability,
「無 常の雰圍氣」「無常の匂ひ」。

Page 16

line 2. the rushes.「木賊」は scouring rushes なれど
scouring の語は普通用ひぬ故略す。

10. registered,「屆書を出した」。
under the heading「項目の下に」。

15. a furlong or two,「一、二丁」。

25. this side of the temple gate ,「山門の手前に」。

Page 17.

line 3. a little white tablet,「白木の小さい墓標」。

13. aging,「古びる」。

VI

Page 18.

line 2. altogether,「總(すべ) て」「前後」。

13. silk crepe *haori*,「縮緬の羽織」。

13–14. a crest of three oak leaves ,「三つ柏の絞」。

17. a new acquaintance ,「初見の人」。
tickling,「こ そばゆい」。

18–19. I shrank from being praised,「賛辭に辟易した」。

20. spoke in high terms,「賞讚した」。

Page 19

line 12. Toying with the brass tongs,
「眞鍮の火箸を弄びながら」。

12–13. the ash-filled brazier before her,「彼女の前に置
かれた手焙」。原文には「桐の手焙」とあれど、
brazier には brass の意あれば桐の木
(paulownia) は用ふこと能はず。

24. "agreed"「それでは」(宜しいの意) 。

Page 20

line 5. a wooden image,「木像」。

    6. flushed red,「赤く熱(ほて) つた」。

VII

Page 21

lines 1-2. my breathing became labored,
    「私を息苦しくした」。

    7. at a loss for an answer,「返答に窮する」。

    11. studied her expression,「彼女の氣色をうかつた」。

    16. the first principle,「第一義」。

    16–17. the standard of values for humanity,
    「人間を評價する標準」。

    21. the ravages of time,「時の威力」。

    24. a mere aimless shell, bereft of its soul,
    「たい漫然と生てゐる魂の拔殻」。

    26. the iron grip of circumstance,「境遇の桎梏」。

Page 22

line 3–4. could not reach out my hand to aid,
    「どうすることも出出来ない」
    「手の附けやうのない」。

    10–11. to escort,「見送つて行く」。
      the steps,「沓脱 (くつねぎ)」。

    16–17. too much,「過分」「勿體ない」。

Page 23

line 2. a human and wholesome feeling,
    「人間らしい好い心持」。

VIII

Page 24

line 2. this thorny path of life,「荊棘の多い人生の道」。
    「辿る」とある故「道」を用ふ。

    3. the realm of death,「死の境地」。

5-6. the supreme state of our attainment,
　　　「人間の達し得る最上至高の狀態」。

10. in my one life,「私一代で」。

14. within the bounds of this life ,「此生の許す範圍內」。

21. "If life is so hard.. ,"「もし人生がさほどつらいなら」。

24. the hypodermic needle,「注射の針」。

25-26. on the very verge of his eternal sleep,
　　　「永遠の眠に赴かんとしてゐる際に」。

Page 25

lines 13-14. the two sides of a sheet of paper,「紙の表裏」。

20. bedim, like a dream,「夢のやうに暈(ほか)す」。

Page 26

line 2. my hope and and advice, は
　　　my hope and advice の誤植。

5. an ordinary follower of naturalism,
　　　「凡庸な自然主義者」。

6. half-distrustfully,「半信半疑で」。

IX

Page 27

lines 2-3. High School days ,「高等學校時代」。Higher
　　　School は普通 University の意に用ひらる れば高等
　　　學校は High School と譯する方可なり。

20. was thinking out for himself,
　　　「彼れ一人で考へてゐた」。

25-26. whithersoever our footsteps led us,
　　　「足の向く方へ」。

Page 28

line 12. a student of limited means,「貧書生」。a poor student
　　　は「質書生」又は「頭の悪い生徒」何れにも用ひらる
　　　ゆる ambiguous.

14. broiled salt salmon,「焼いた鹽鮭」。

22. with equanimity,「平氣の平座で」。

Page 29

line 1. for the first time in years,「何年ぶりかで」「久しぶりで」。

6. "You are putting on airs, eh ?"「いやに氣取つてゐるな」「いやに澄ましてゐるな」。

11. a feeling of high exaltation,「すがすがしい氣持」。

X

Page 30

lines 3–4. the traces of our old features,「昔の面影」。

8–9. the old forms,「故(もと)の姿」。

16. side hair,「揉み上げ」。

26. He was wearing a loose mantled overcoat,
「彼はとんびのやうな外套をぶわぶわに着てゐた」。

Page 31

line 1. hanging to a strap in the car,
「電車の中で釣革にぶらさがりながら」。

9. "I shouldn't be surprised, "「さうかも知れない」。
perhaps so の意。

24. gold-rimmed glasses,「金緣眼鏡」。

Page 32

line 1. reading glasses ,「老眼鏡」。
spectacles for the aged 等と譯しては不可。

10. Master,「達人」。

13–14. bound in with ice and snow,
「雪と氷に鎖ざされた」。

XI

Page 33

lines 15–16. became distasteful,「厭になつて来た」。

4. made no headway,「埒があかなかつた」。

Page 34

lines 2–3. the leaden sky, from which a gloomy rain seemed about to fall,
「佗びしい雨が今にも降り出しさうな灰色の空」。

17. only that part of you that is disguised,
「貴方の伴はつた所ばかりを」。

23. an opening, 「隙(すき)」。

Page 35

lines 2–3. all social amenities, 「社交上の巧言令色」。

13. the status quo, 「現狀」。

XII

Page 36

lines 2–3. the customary paper strip, 「短冊」。

14. I proved unequal to the task, it was too much for me.
「實際弱らせられた」。

26. stuck in, 「挟み込んだ」。

Page 37

line 2. to put away, 「仕舞ふ」。

12. his insistence, 「彼の催促」。

27. to autograph the picture with some comment,
「畫の賛を書く」。

XIII

Page 39

lines 5–6. the Loyal Samurai, 「義士」「四十七士」。

9. began to pester me, began to bother me,
「私をくるしめ出した。

23. it would bemean myself,
「自分の品格を傷つけるやうで」。

Page 40

lines 1–2. My feelings .. grew ruffled,
「私の感情は・・・荒(すさ)んで来た」。

11. the man .. was unperturbed,
「其の男は・・・平氣であつた」。

25. the Ward Office,「區役所」。

Page 41

line 1. on that account,「それが爲めに」。double the postage,
「倍の郵税」。twice over,「二度」。

3. perhas は perhaps の誤植。

8. a bit gratifying,「一寸喜ばせた」「感心させたので」。

11. on the plea,「口實」。

XIV

Page 42

line 6. the boisterous period,
「騒々しい時代」「八釜ましい頃」。

7. royalists,「勤王黨」feudalists,「佐幕黨」。

9. in order to wash her hands,
「手を洗ふために」。これだけで十分「小用」の意
あれば、常に「小用云々」は斯く譯すべし。

11–12. stood forcefully, as if pressing back the wall,
「壁を壓し付ける様な勢で立つてゐた」。

24. double lidded eyes ,「二重瞼の眼」。

Page 43

line 5. the square aperture,「四角に切つた孔」。

8. dark lanterns,「籠燈提灯」。

26–27. “ You women talk too much,”「女といふ者は餘
計な事をいふものだ」。原文「餘計な事をいふ女
だ」の譯 You are the woman who talks too much,
なれど、前者の方が餘りに廣く用ひらるためこれ
を探る。

Page 44

line 6. they complimented us,「賞めてくれた」。

13. the point of a drawn sword,「拔身の尖端」。

16. came through,「濟んだ」。、

18. over the tea cups ,「茶受話に」。

XV

Page 45

line 5. ceremonial cord,「水引」。

   6. two five yen bills ,「五圓札二枚」。bills, bank notes .

   14. according to the world standard,「世間の通り相場では」。

   16. money with no gratitude attached,
       「有難味の附着してるない金」。

   17-18. I feel far better not to receive such a token of
       gratitude,「斯うした御禮を受けない方が餘程颯
       爽してるる」。

   23. out of kindness,「好意づくで」。

   27. for a certain fee,「これこれの御禮をするが」。

Page 46

line 16. I have managed to get through each day as it came,
   「今日まで過して来てるる」。

   21-22. the margin left me for working in behalf of others,
      「私が他人の為めに働いてやるといふ餘地」。

   26. held my ground,
      「自分の陣地を固持した」「強情であつた」。

Page 47

line 10. I may be conceited,「私の己惚かも知れませんが」。

   12. the general run of the students, the majority of the
   students.

   21. think it over,「熟慮する」。

XVI

Page 48

line 15. clipping with scissors,
   「鋏をちよきちよきと鳴らし」。

   19. by plying his scissors,「鋏をせつせと動かして」。
      plying は using の意。

   23. patronized me,「私を最負にして下すった」。

Page 49

line 13. many congratulatory gifts,「方々からの御祝物」。

21. assignation houses,「待合」。assignation, an
appointment to meet, used mostly in a bad sense.

24. a sock store「足袋屋」。

XVII

Page 51

lines 6-7. whiling away his time,
「なまけてゐた」「(家で) ごろごろしてるた」。

10. for little or nothing,「二足三文に」。

11. bundled over, into my cousin's house,
「從兄の家に轉がり込んでるた」。

19. were hailed,「聲をかけられた」。

26. the general trend of things,
「(といつた) 風の調子で(あつた) 」。

Page 52

line 14. duck cloth,「小倉地」。

20. underwaist,「襦袢」。waist, the bodice of a
woman's dress.

Page 53

line 4. a respectable matron,「品の好い奥様」。

XVIII

Page 54

lines 3-4. everything about me is awry,
「自分の周圍のものがごちゃごちゃしてみる」「きち
んと片付かない」。awry, disordered.

14. I failed to make out, I was unable to understand.

22. was naturally beyond me,
「無論私には分らなかつた」「通じなかつた」。

XIX

Page 57

lines 4–5. a traveler's stopping place, 「宿場」。

    8. an out-of-the-way corner, 「邊鄙な隅」。

    19–20. a great measure of wine , 「桝酒」。

    21. the measure, 「其の桝」

Page 58

line 8. a pole-maker's, 「棒屋」。

    14. to speak of intimacy, 「交際からいふと」。that was
        that intimacy.

    25. "How much am I offered?" 「若干?」。

Page 59

line 5. the bean-curd seller, 「豆腐屋」。

    10–11. measurably high, 「可なり高い」「小高い」。

    17–18. chilled my boyish spirit,
        「小さい私の心を塞くした」。

XX

Page 60

lines 8–9. the fire chief of the ward, 「町内の鳶頭」。

    11. the coat with red lined insignia,
        「赤い筋入りの印袢纏」。slipped on,
        「突つ掛けて」。insignia, emblem.

    14–15. took a husband into the family, 「養子を貰つた」。

    18. some ward office, 「或る區役所」。

    20. the hall, 「席塲」「寄席」。

Page 61

line 14. the rice paddies, 「水田」。

    22. as if the sky were overcast, as if the sky were clouded.

Page 62

lines 1–2. fair weather clogs, 「日和下駄」。

    3. the thaw there, 「そこの霜溶」。
        但し thaw は「雪溶」にも用ふ。

8. true to form, according to rule,
　　形式にたがはず」「型の如く」。

XXI

Page 63

lines 7–8. lived in such a style, lived in so ostentatious a way.

19–20. the covered boat,「屋根船」。

25. ... gives me food for recalling, ...「回顧の種になる」。

Page 64

lines 4–5. the theatre-tea-house,「芝居茶屋」。

7. the high pit ,「高土間」。

15. figured silk kimono,
　　「縮緬の模様のある着物」。

23–24. for the sake of caution,
　　「要心までに」「無要心だからと云つて」。

Page 65

line 6. had to put on style
　　「派出にしなければならなかつた」。

10. his lady love,「馴染の女」。

13. my third elder brother, my third eldest brother
　　の誤植。

19. a dignified portico at the entrance,
　　「嚴めしい式臺の付いた玄關」。

21. on the stoop, 式臺を上つた所。

22. punitive instruments,「成敗の道具」。

XXII

Page 66

lines 1–2. one spell of sickness, one period of sickness, or one
　　attack of illness.

15. black-bordered cards, mourning cards, death notices,
　　「黒枠のついた刷物」。

23. the span of human life,「人間の短い壽命」。

Page 67

line 5. listening to the ritual service,
「讀經に耳傾けながら」。

11. a man who had been through the war,
「戰爭に出た経験のある人」。

21. their turn,「彼等の順番」

25. frame of mind, state of mind.

Page 68

line 11. More often than not, quite often.

17. playing a trick on me,「私を愚弄して」。

XXIII

Page 69

line 4. folks, people.

12. give my mind free play,
「自分の心を自由に遊ばせる」。

26. Headman,「名主」。

26. Ward Chief,「區長」。

Page 70

line 4. indulge in a smile,「た微笑する」。

17. I was out house-hunting, I was out in search of a
house.

25. looked in at the front,「表から覗いた」。

Page 71

line 6. stood blankly,「茫然と佇立してるた」。

15. a rude enclosure,「疎らな圍ひ」。

17. seemed dwarfed,「畸形兒の様であつた」。

XXIV

Page 72

line 4. in one way and another, by someway or other.

13. in the equinoctial festival time,「お彼岸の祭に」。

15. satiated,「滿足した」「けんなりした」。

18. without any anxiety, は without any anxiety
    の misprint.

24–25. I cannot escape many thoughts, I cannot avoid
    thinking many things.「色々思 ひ當る事がある」。

Page 73

line 11. sipping,「啜りながら」。

12. rehearsed, told in detail,「語つてきかせた」。

13. was in employ,「雇はれてるた」「使用人であつた」。

14–15. was not of the laity,「素人ではなかつた」。

15–16. She took her own life, she put an end to her life .

18. mistress, 此處にては悪い意味で「圍る者」。昔は此
    の語三様の意義に川ひられしも、現今にては「
    主婦」然らざれば「圍るもの」の二様しか用ひら
    れず。

19. to buy her off ,「受け出す」。

20. to have made friends with,「味方にして」。
    her matron,「老妓」。

Page 74

line 5. "Maybe so", it may be so.

13. amorous words.「艶つほい言葉」。

XXV

Page 75

lines 7–8. the first little street this side,
    「一つ手前の小さい通り」。

11–12. a steel-blue hue,「鐵御納戸の」。

15–16. the cleats of my clogs,「足駄の歯」。

21. corrode,「腐蝕する」。

22. mien,「(顔の)様子」。

25. a covered rikisha,「幌俥(ほろぐるま)」。

Page 76

line 6. was carried away,「見惚(みと) れてるた」。

22. my words at their face value,「私の言葉を其儘に」。

Page 77

lines 8–9. deep in the recesses of my memory,
　　　　「私の記憶の奥底ふかく」。

XXVI

Page 78

lines 4–5. went through his property,
　　　　「財産を無くした」「家を潰した」。

　　　6. lived off me, lived at my expense; sponged on me,
　　　　「私の所の食客になつてゐた」。

　　18–19. on the edge of Shiba,「芝の外れに」。

　　20. care-free existence,「呑気な生活」。

Page 79

line 5. hard-wood desks ,「硬木で造つた机」「上等の机」。
　　　hard-wood は轉じて
　　　high grade wood の意に用ひらる。

　　13. a sine qua non, an essential ,「なくてならぬ者」。

　　21. so I have to, so I have to deliver letters.

Page 80

line 9. a laughing stock,「笑ひの種」。

　　16–17. to take it up, to begin it.

XXVII

Page 81

lines 4–5. the theatrical conventions,
　　　　「演藝上の習慣、約束」。

　　　6. the ability to merge myself,
　　　　　「自分を同化せしめる能力」。

　　12. a half-sitting posture,「中腰」。

　　18. "Think of it as I will,"「どう考へても」。

Page 82

line 18. differentiation,「差別」。

Page 83

line 4. took up my cudgels, came to my defense,
「私の議論を引き受けた」。

6–7. inarticulate, 「呂律の廻りかねる」「へべれけ」。

XXVIII

Page 84

line 2. what generation, 「何代」。

9. the second in line, the second in succession,
「二番目」。

15. trample upon, 「踏みにぢる」。

18. treatment, 「手當て」。

19. jet black, 「眞つ黒」。

Page 85

line 3. much to my annoyance,
「私を隨分な目に逢はせて」。

4. contracted, was attacked by.

7. scabs, 「瘡蓋」。

18. out of pity for it, feeling pity for it.

26–27. had no margin of strength for thinking,
「考へる餘裕さへ出なかつた」。

Page 86

line 6. recuperated, regained strength.

XXIX

Page 87

lines 6-7. sent me away to be brought up,
「私を里子にやつてしまつた」。

8. foster home, 「養家」。

12. Tucked, 「入れ込まれて」。

12–13. odds and ends of furniture, 「がらくた道具」。

18. roundly, severely.

22. pretty sure, quite sure.

24. the age of discretion, arrived at years of judgment,「物心のつく頃」。

Page 88

lines 6–7. kept their faces unconcerned,「澄ました顔をしてゐた」。

15. openly,「あからさまに」「著しく」。

17. in my folly,「馬鹿な私」。

XXX

Page 90

line 20. relapses ,「再發」。

Page 91

line 6. There is no telling, no one knows.

19–20. with a great report,「大きな音を發して」。

26. come to such a pass,「さういふ破目に陷る」。

Page 92

lines 7–8. eventuate,「終結する」「曲折してゆく」。

XXXI

Page 93

lines 2–3. a chum, an intimate acquaintance.

元は slang なりしも今は一般に用ひらる。

9. rendezvous, 此處にては

meeting の意なれど、時 として
the place of meeting の意にも用ひらる。

9. a stationary shop 又は單に

a stationer にて「文房具屋」。

17–18. came under the suspicion of counterfeiting,「質金を造つたといふ嫌疑を受けて」。

25–26. never gave a thought to,

「考へてみるといふ事は全然なかつた」
「考へた事は一度もなかつた」。

Page 94

line 5. by looking them up, by searching for them.

    6. entry ,「入口」「玄關」。

    10–11. turned the pages over aimlessly here and there, 「其處此處を引つ繰返して見た」。

    12. what they were about,「何の事が書いてある のか」。

Page 95

line 2. to bargain him down,「價切る」俗語。[*Originally translated as* "Jew him down."]

    9. elated over the matter,「それを嬉しがつて」。

XXXII

Page 96

line 2. came ambling in,「ぶらりと遣つて来た」。

    4. remained hesitant,「愚圖愚圖してゐた」。

    11. turned them over to,「渡した」。

    19. began to dawn upon me, I began to recall them.

Page 97

line 16. pin money, pocket money.

Page 98

line 1. It was more than I could stand, It was more than I could endure.

    10. I say you can have them,「遣らうといふんだよ」。

    11. to have them, to possess them.

XXXIII

Page 99

line 6. more complicated dealings, 「もつと込み入つた取引き、懸合」。

    14. sneered at behind my back,「蔭で馬鹿にされた」。

    19. unconscionable liars,「擦れ枯らしの嘘吐」。

       from the very start, from the very beginning.

    26. a bold face,「厚顔」。

Page 100

line 1. to adjust,「適應させる」「片付ける」。

9. aptly fits,「ぴつたりと合ふ」。

10. the delicate line,「微妙な線」。

10–11. without deviating the fraction of an inch,
　　　「寸分の間違ひもなく」。

13. Not counting my prejudice,「私の僻は除外して」。

23. given me from above, given me from Heaven.

Page 101

lines 1–2. one stratum of society,
　　「社會のある階級」「社食の一部分」。

10. dubious intuition,「あやふやな直覺」。

<h1 align="center">XXXIV</h1>

Page 102

lines 5–6. they couldn't understand you,
　　　they could not understand what you had said.

23. couldn't get that, could not understand that.

Page 103

line 1. time and again, many times.

Page 104

line 4. pressing problem, insistent problem,
　　　「目前に逼つた問題」。

15. in refutation of the statement,
　　　　「述べた事の反證」。

16. to dispel the disappointment,
　　　　「失望を打ち消す」。

20. my own density,「私の不明」。

22. rectified my mistake, corrected my mistake.

XXXV

Page 105

lines 5–6. a sign announcing the day performance,
「晝席の看板」。

6–7. a short half cho,「小半丁」。

8–9. dealt with romantic affairs only,
「色物だけをかけた」。
romantic affairs,「花やかなもの」「色もの」。
never set foot there, never entered there .

18. an air of respectability,「上品な風、氣分」。

19. low lattice partitions,「低い格子の仕切」。

20. the regular patrons,「定連」。

23. the well curb,「井桁」。

25. with no feeling of restriction,
「窮屈な感じのしない」。

27. a detached villa ,「離れ屋」「離れ座敷」。

Page 106

line 2. had spare time on their hands,
「使ひ切れぬほど時間に餘裕のある」。

3. with ennui,「怠屈さうに」「呑氣さうに」。
hair pincers,「毛拔」。

14. a tacit understanding,「無言の規約」。

18–19. an open-hearted and care-free spirit,
「隠しだてをしない太つ腹で呑気な氣風」。

24. once checked clogs somewhere,
「以前何處かで下足番をした」。
to check clogs,「下駄に札をつける、下足番をす
る」。

Page 107

line 6. a year-end meeeting,「年末の會」「忘年會」。

21. appeared in Nanryu's intermission,
「南龍の中入前をつとめた」。

XXXVI

Page 108

lines 13–14. the feeling that they might not approach without cause, 「相當の理由なくして、無暗に近寄れないと云つた風の感じ」。

23. brought up, as he was, in Tokyo, (he) having been brought up in Tokyo.

Page 109

lines 1–2. extremely conscientious,
「非常に几帳面で」「四角四面で」。

always assumed a strict demeanor,
常に舉止が嚴格であつた」「始終堅苦しく構へてるた」。

6. began to soften, began to become effeminate,
「にやけて来た」。

7–8. got to going out, formed the habit of going out, 「宅(うち) を外にしはじめた」。

8–9. an old taffeta kimono, 「古渡唐棧の着物」。
stiff girdle, 「角帶」。

12. imitating the voice of the professional,
「本職(くろうと)の口真似をする」「假聲を遣ふ」。

15–16. an opponent, 「相手」。

21–22. If my memory does not fail me, if I remember correctly.

23–24. the night after cremation past,
「逮夜も済んだ」。

Page 110

line 5. remained single, remained unmarried.

11. ashes had been interred, 「遺骨の埋められた」。

13. had relations with her, 「女と關係があつた」。

18–19. withered and hardened to a crust,
「しなび乾いて殻(から) のやうになつた」。

XXXVII

Page 111

line 3. but little material, only little material.

11–12. call up from the now long ago, call up that which
has now become dim past,
「今は遠い過去から呼び起す」。

13. Born as I was in her later years, though I was born in
her later years.

26. lithographs, 「石摺りもの」。

Page 112

line 4. silk gauze kimono, 「絽の帷子(かたびら) 」。

4–5. a black satin girdle, 「黒繻子の帶」。

20. a pawnbroker , 「質屋」。

21. godowns, 「藏(くら) 」。

Page 113

line 4. a matter almost beyond my grasp,
「取り留めようのない事實」。

10. old colour prints, 「昔の錦繪」。

11. a red back, は a red silk back
と訂正す、「(着物の) 紅絹裏」。

14–15. by no stretch of the imagination can I recall,
「どんなに想像しても眼に浮かばない」。

18–19. a bed covering, a quilt.
「寢臺にかけるもの」「布團」。

XXXVIII

Page 114

line 2. long since, long ago .

5. a beautiful writing box は a beautiful lettercase
と訂正す。a letter-case, 「文箱」a writing box,
「硯箱」。embossed lacquer, 「高蒔繪」。

8. I am penning this, I am writing this.

13. to get along, to live on.

19. headstrong, willful, obstinate, 「強情な」。

Page 115

1. cranky, ill-natured,「氣むづかしい」俗語。

    9. square written characters,
        「楷書で書かれた字」。script,「草書」。

   19. continue は continue の misprint.

Page 116

2. used up, spent.

    4. no way of making it good, no way of compensating for
        it,「どうしても償へない」。

   12. came right upstairs, came straightway upstairs,
      「すぐ二階へ上って来た」。

XXXIX

Page 117

line 3. felt relaxation,「氣を許した」。

   6–7. soft boiled egg, half-boiled egg,「半熟の鶏卵」。
     「半熟の鶏卵を食べて」に續く原文廿字は
     English の convention に從つて譯を省略す。

   10–11. discarded charcoal bags ,「不要の炭俵」。

   14–15. "That won't do," that will not do for me, I don't
       like that,「いやあーだ」。

   23. giving my soul free play,「魂を自由に遊ばせて」。

   25. the potted orchid ,「鉢植の蘭」。

Page 118

line 13. Riding upon this assault,「此の攻撃の上に乗つて」。

   20. in jumbled fashion,「ごちゃごちやに」。

   25. take all the color out of it,「全く色氣を取り除く」。

Page 119

lines 9–10. looking out upon the race in general,
     「一般の人類を見渡しながら」。
      wreathed in smiles ,「破顔一笑」。

   16. as if to recall it now and then,
      「折々思ひ出したやうに」

Editorial Notes

The preceding Notes are by the translators Iwao Matsuhara and E. T. Iglehart, with the exception of the change made at page 95, line 2. Page and line numbers have been adjusted to conform to this edition.

The following notes are intended to help readers that may be unfamiliar with some names, dates, or aspects of Japanese culture.

9   *furoshiki*] cloth used for wrapping goods in transit

16   Yamaga Soko] (1622–1685) Military strategist and Confucian philosopher who described the mission and obligations of the samurai class. His grave is at the Sōtō Zen temple of Sōsan-ji in Shinjuku, Tokyo.

17   that of our cat] Described in the essay "Our Cat's Grave".

23   Euraku] The Yūraku-za was a Western-style theatre opened in Tokyo in 1908.

28   Saghalien] Sakhalin Island off the east coast of Russia. Occupied by Japan and Russia intermittently since 1807, the southern half was ceded to Japan in 1905 following the Russo-Japanese War.

28   Akita to Yokote] Cities on the northwest coast of Honshu

42   about the time I was born] Natsume Kinnosuke was born in 1867.

45   two five yen bills] Ten yen was approximately $5 in 1915, worth around $150 today (2025).

47   Iwasaki or Mitsui] Iwasaki Yatarō (1835–1885), Japanesee industrialist, founder of Mitsubishi;

and Mitsui Takatoshi (1622–1694), founder of the
Mitsui family, the richest in Japan.

57   Yedo] Or Edo, former name of Tokyo, changed in 1868.

57   Yasubei Horibe] (1670–1703) Famous samurai
swordsman who killed three opponents in a duel
at Takada-no-Baba. He was later among the Forty-
seven Rōnin.

57   *Naga-uta*] Traditional music played on the shamisen, a
three-stringed instrument.

58   *"Tabi no koromo wa suzu-gake no."*] "The travel robe
of the wandering monk." From the Noh plays
Kurozuka and *Ataka*, or kabuki plays based on
them.

62   Shiki] Masaoka Shiki (1867–1902) Japanese poet,
essayist, and literary critic; considered one of the
masters of the haiku form.

64   Tanosuke] Sawamura Tanosuke III (1845–1878)

64   Tossho] The actor Suketakaya Takasuke IV was known
as Sawamura Tosshô II from 1854 to 1879.

65   Itchu Bushi] Style of shamisen music developed by
Miyako Itchu (b.1650).

65   *Genkan*] entrance

66   an earlier death] Natsume Sōseki died December 9,
1916, aged 49.

68   this Newspaper] These essays appeared in the Tokyo
Asahi Shimbun and Osaka *Asahi Shimbun*
newspapers.

69   the four characters *Ki, Ku, I, Cho*] 気く井町

76 Ōtsuka Kusuo] (1875–1910) Poet and novelist, former student of Natsume. She was the author of the anti-war poem *Ohyakudo Moude* (One Hundred Visits to Shrine, 1905) and the story *Shinobine* ("A Faint Tune", 1897).

79 Goodrich's English History] *A Pictorial History of England* by Samuel G. Goodrich (1793–1860) was first published in 1846.

80 in good Japanese: 'Thank you, you are alright'] "Arigatō, daijōbudayo" (ありがとう、大丈夫だよ).

81 Jakuchu] Itō Jakuchū (1716–1800) Japanese painter of the mid-Edo period.

94 Nampo Ota ... Shoku-San-Jin] (1749–1823) Japanese poet and fiction writer; Shokusanjin was one of several pennames he used.

94 fifty sen] or half a yen; about 25 cents US at the time; roughly equivalent to $10 today (2025).

107 Shin-Tomi-Za] Kabuki theatre in Tokyo, built in 1878.

109 tōhachi hand game] Also known as *kitsuneken*, a game of 2 opponents and three gestures meaning village headman, hunter and fox. Headman defeats hunter who defeats fox who defeats headman; like rock-paper-scissors.

112 godown] a warehouse or storage building

Natsume Sōseki's house in Waseda (1916).

Natsume Sōseki on the verandah in 1915.